"I confess to thee, O Father, Lord of heaven and earth, because thou hast hid these things from the wise and prudent, and hast revealed them to little ones."

—Matthew 11:25

Venerable Anne de Guigné
1911-1922

ANNE

THE LIFE OF
VENERABLE ANNE DE GUIGNÉ
1911-1922

By

A Benedictine Nun of
Stanbrook Abbey

*"Suffer the little children to come
unto me, and forbid them not; for of
such is the kingdom of God."*
—Mark 10:14

TAN BOOKS AND PUBLISHERS, INC.
Rockford, Illinois 61105

NIHIL OBSTAT: Dom Justin McCann, O.S.B.
                 Censor Deputatus
                 January 8, 1932

IMPRIMATUR: ✠ W. E. Kelly, O.S.B.
                 Abbot Praes.

NIHIL OBSTAT: Bernard Griffin, S.T.D.
                 Censor Deputatus

IMPRIMATUR: ✠ Thomas
                 Archbishop of Birmingham
                 Birmingham
                 August 20, 1932

First published in 1932 by Burns, Oates & Washbourne, Ltd, London. Retypeset and republished in 1997 by TAN Books and Publishers, Inc. with permission of Stanbrook Abbey.

Grateful acknowledgments to the Freundeskreis Maria Goretti e.V., Munich, for use of the pictures on pages 22 and 28 and Afterword material.

Library of Congress Catalog Card No.: 97-60765

ISBN 0-89555-599-9

Printed and bound in the United States of America.

TAN BOOKS AND PUBLISHERS, INC.
P.O. Box 424
Rockford, Illinois 61105
1997

"Obedience is the sanctity of children."

—*Motto of Anne's*
First Communion
retreat
(See page 18)

"Anne never stopped to think whether a thing was pleasant or not if she knew it was the will of God, either for some reason of duty or necessity, or for the good of others. Her will ruled all her actions so that there was perfect order in her life. . . ."

—*Mother St. Raymond,*
Anne's teacher
(See page 80)

CONTENTS

DECLARATION OF OBEDIENCE

PREFACE
To the 1932 Edition

THIS is the life of Anne de Guigné,[1] a little girl who died only ten years ago. A short and uneventful life as the world views things, but full of very great events in the eyes of God, who seems to wish that we should know how important she is in the world above, for He allows her to "spend her Heaven doing good upon earth."

The facts are taken from the French book *Anne de Guigné* by Rev. Fr. Etienne Lajeunie, O.P., supplemented by the original depositions written by the child's mother and by her governess, Mlle. B. The Countess de Guigné has corrected various details while reading the manuscript of this book and most kindly supplied the photographs.

Considerable use has also been made of the depositions of the late Mother St. Raymond, a nun of the Auxiliatrice convent at Cannes, who taught the catechism class which Anne attended each year when the family went south for the winter.

The diocesan or "informative" Process, preparatory to Anne's Beatification, commenced some months ago, when the Bishop of Annecy, Msgr. du Bois' de la Villerabel, received official authoriza-

---

1. Guigné is pronounced *Geen yay.*—*Publisher,* 1997.

tion from the Sacred Congregation of Rites. The
Bishop is himself President of the Tribunal, with
Msgr. Hertzog as Postulator of the Cause in Rome,
and Canon J. Mugnier, professor at the Grand Sem-
inaire in Annecy, as Vice-Postulator.

The document from Rome was dated Christmas
Day, 1931. It seems as if the Christ Child wished
to show that He has taken His little friend by the
hand, so that she may pass safely through the courts
of Rome, where nursery Saints are rare.

It should be mentioned, however, that an occa-
sional use of the word "Saint" is not intended to
anticipate in any way the future judgement of the
Church. This applies also to the account of various favors attributed to Anne's intercession. All
that is here written is a plain statement of facts
which the Church will judge in God's own time.

See also the Afterword, p. 117.

ANNE

"There will be saints among the children."

—Pope St. Pius X

Chapter 1

FINDING THE WAY

IT was the 30th of July, 1915; the second year of the war.

For one four-year-old girl, this was "the Day of the Lord, great and exceedingly bitter."

Is it possible to speak of a great and bitter day in the life of a child of four? It is certainly not usual, but this book is about a child who was not usual.

On that July morning Anne awoke to see her mother standing by the bed, and her mother's eyes were red from a night of tears. Three times in this one year of war the child's father had returned wounded—now, "Daddy is dead." And the sword went down into the little one's soul "even unto the division of the spirit." This is the absolute truth. It was a dividing point. Behind lay an ordinary childhood, full of promise but stained by many faults. After it came the maturity of holiness.

There are several ways of climbing the mountain of sanctity. Anne's way was to attempt the face of the cliff. She went straight up, for her time was short. God called her to come up the quickest way, and she came.

*   *   *

Who was this child? Her family called her
Nenette, but she had a good supply of other names
besides. Jeanne, Marie, Josephine, Anne, all these
had been lavished on the eldest daughter of Jacques,
Count de Guigné and his wife, Antoinette de
Charette.

Anne's birth on April 25, 1911, was followed a
year later by that of the son and heir, Jacques or
Jojo; and then came two little sisters, Madeleine
and Marie Antoinette, whose long names soon
became shortened to Leleine and Marinette.

Their home was the stately Chateau de la Cour
overlooking the Lake of Annecy. "We have as fine
a chateau as anyone," Anne once remarked in a
moment of weakness. Certainly it was a home worth
loving and a little girl might perhaps be forgiven for
boasting of it. That part of Savoy is lovely beyond
description, and the chateau stands on a height with
all the beauty of the lake spread out below.

This was Anne's home and here she lived all her
life except for a few months each winter when the
family went to their house in Cannes.

Some Saints' biographers gravely assure us that
they "showed every sign of sanctity from earliest
infancy"! Anne can hardly be said to have done
that. In many ways she was a dear child, very loving, intelligent and perfectly frank, but also a most
tempestuous little person with an iron will when
there was question of getting her own way. She
may in fact be said to have shown every sign of
naughtiness from earliest infancy!

A doctor can testify that there were no signs of precocious sanctity to be seen in the very troublesome baby he had to deal with. The child was sufficiently ill to cause anxiety and it was imperative to examine her. But Anne did not like the doctor, or perhaps his instruments frightened her. In any case she immediately became a miniature windmill with her arms and legs very busy all at once, and when the doctor tried to hold them: "Take your hat and go!" came the furious command from the crib. The little lady could hardly speak plainly yet, but she knew how to make herself understood. Such scenes were not at all unusual.

There is a photograph taken when she was about three years old which gives a good idea of her character at this time. Eyes, mouth and chin, all are very hard. There is frankness in the little face and courage, great courage, and the power of great love; but self-will is clearly written there. It is the face of one who will follow none but herself.

Anne was in fact a born leader, but during these first four years of her life she was also a little tyrant. Among other children she not only led but *drove*. Ordinarily, they were usually glad enough to follow, for there was something very attractive about her and she was full of invention and enterprise; but if anybody showed resistance, there was trouble. The tyrant instinct rose, and she carried all before her, even physically sometimes if she had strength enough!

One summer when she was only three years old, Anne was playing with a boy cousin a little older

than herself. After some time they came across a
large heap of sand. "Let's climb on top," suggested
the little girl, suiting the action to the word, but
the boy held back.

"No, I won't," he said, "it's too high."

"But I say you must," retorted his little cousin.
"You *shall* come up, I'll make you!" and she began
to pull and tug. It was a fine fight, but the little
girl was winning when their nurse arrived on the
scene and separated the pair. Anne could not have
won by strength of arm, but her violence frightened the bigger child. It was a battle of wills. Surely
she too had trembled at the thought of balancing
on top of that heap of crumbling sand which
seemed so high to a three-year-old, but if Anne
meant to do a thing, fear would never stop her.

About the same time, she and her cousins were
taken to see a menagerie. Anne was younger than
any of the others, but as usual she took command
of the group. "Come along," her aunt heard her
say to one considerably larger than herself, "I'll lift
you up to pat the giraffe!" She was quite serious
about it.

All these things showed that there was a power
in the child; but how would she use it? Her mother
wondered and prayed and "kept all these words in
her heart."

Anne's heart was the best part of her. She was
really wonderfully loving. But here again there was
a shadow to the picture, for she was also jealous.
She did not love the brother who had succeeded
her in the cradle. She wanted the whole of her

mother's attention; her father's, too, of course, but particularly her mother's, and now a new baby was sitting on Mother's lap. It was certainly very hard, unbearable in fact, so Anne came up one day with a handful of sand which she began to rub into the baby's eyes. It was not fun, very far from it. She wanted to make Jacques cry because her mother had kissed him.

Fortunately this did not last long, for like most children Anne soon found that a real live baby is much nicer than a doll, and the little sisters who followed had a much better welcome. She began to find it rather pleasant to be the eldest.

She was nearly four when the youngest was born, and she immediately appropriated the new baby as her own property. Marinette had chosen to arrive on the 4th of January in the midst of an unusually severe spell of cold weather, so the bishop gave leave for the little one to be baptized in the house. It was a great day for Anne; she felt she had "come of age," in fact, for her mother decided that she should be allowed to stand as godmother. Feeling full of importance she made the responses very gravely; but what most impressed her was the fact that she was now responsible for Marinette's welfare. This was very much to Anne's taste, and she did not stop to distinguish between spiritual and temporal care! No one in the house had a chance of forgetting that the baby had a godmother. All that day Anne hovered about, trying to get hold of her spiritual charge, and at last succeeded in reaching the crib when the nurse was not looking.

But good nurses have eyes in the backs of their heads, and this one looked around in time to catch the godmother just as she was getting the baby into her arms.

"My darling, you mustn't touch her. Little girls can't look after babies!"

Anne drew herself up with dignity: "They can on a Baptism day," she retorted. "I'm her god-mother."

But the nurse was obdurate and the crestfallen little godmother had to retire, vanquished for once.

It had been a happy day for Anne, but her mother was sad, for it was 1915 and the Count de Guigné was not there to see his new little daughter.

At the first outbreak of war, he had rejoined his old regiment, the Chasseurs Alpins, from which he had retired at his marriage for family reasons. He was still quite young, and by 1914 his life was a very busy one, for he had thrown himself into most things that were worth doing, especially the Catholic activities of the district. He was inter-ested in many branches of study too; he lectured, he wrote, and what is not quite so common, he thought deeply and he prayed.

It was a happy life, congenial and full, not easy therefore to leave, but Jacques de Guigné laid it down at the first call of duty and left for the front.

The little family was not long alone. In a month their father was home again, wounded. It was not a very severe injury, however, and before long he was able to get around a little with the help of crutches. Anne took her wounded father very seriously. She quite understood that Daddy had come home to be looked after, and looking after people was very much in her line, so she made up her mind to be his nurse. There were usually too many grown up people around for her to have a chance of doing much, but every now and then she found him alone and could play "nurse" to her heart's content. She trotted around full of importance, fetching him books and arranging his cushions. Sometimes she was even seen staggering along with his big crutches, though they were about twice as long as herself. The other children were really too small to understand much, so here at least Anne had the field to herself.

Very soon, however, Lieut. de Guigné went back to his regiment, only to return a few days later wounded more severely. This time he might legitimately have taken a fairly long leave, but he felt his duty was with his men and insisted on hurrying back with his wounds still open. In February he was wounded again, so seriously that he was sent to the hospital at Lyons for an operation. Here Madame de Guigné went to see him, taking Anne with her.

It was a strange experience for the tiny child. She stood gazing at the long line of white beds, strangely awed by the sense of suffering all around. There was no playing at nurse here. Her mother told her that all these poor men were suffering for France—her father, too. It was a great thought. Dimly she began to realize what life was about.

But Anne's father was a brave and strong man.

He got the better of his wounds again, and on the 3rd of May, feast of the Holy Cross, he said good-bye to his home for the last time and went back to the horrors he knew too well.

This time God asked for the supreme sacrifice. The Count de Guigné was ready. With a smile on his lips to the priest who had given him absolution, he led his men to the attack and fell, mortally wounded at last.

The news reached the poor widow four days later on July 28. That night she grieved alone while the little orphans slept, but next morning she rose and went to her eldest child.

Of St. Thérèse of Lisieux it is said that the sun shone on her joy and the rain came with her tears, but it was not so for Anne. The glory of a perfect summer's day shone upon her grief. Was it the irony of nature? At the time it may have seemed so, but the Lord of nature knew that this day her glory had begun, for the light of grace poured in through her open wound and lit up the child's life. It was right that the sun should shine.

Anne was no longer the same. She looked long and thoughtfully at her mother's sad eyes. How much did she understand? Who can say? A little child's mind is hard to read. But she knew that in dying we pass out of this world to God. Did she know that we can "die powerfully"? Probably not; but we know it, for even the blind and "slow of heart" can hardly fail to see that the father's willing sacrifice drew down a flood of grace on his little daughter. From the day of his death it seemed as if all his virtues had fallen to her as an inheritance, and we know too that she worked with the gift of God till it brought forth the hundredfold; but in this world the mysteries of grace can be seen only dimly, "in a dark manner." The full story is written in the Book of Life.

Anne was a practical little soul. She realized now that to reach God we must please Him and to please Him we must be good and that the surest way for a little girl to be good is by pleasing her mother. So she set to work first of all to comfort her mother in every way she could. All day long she tried to be thoughtful and to remember the things she had been told to do—and tried to make the others remember too, for the old instinct of command was not dead! If she herself had started on the way of perfection, she meant to carry them all along with her.

"You *must* be good, Jojo, because Mother is sad," she used to whisper to her noisy little brother, who was more inclined to listen now that there were no more tempers to be feared from Nenette. The children were too young to realize that there was a change in their sister, but they began to love her more and turned to her for everything. "Anne always knows how to arrange things," Jojo would say; and she did, but now it was usually at her own expense. All she thought of was how to please the others, so of course there were no more tempers nor selfishness, because she no longer wanted to get her own way but to make them happy, and above all to keep them good. But this was hard

work for the poor little girl, though scarcely anyone guessed it.

The new governess who arrived in January 1916
certainly never suspected anything of the kind. She
was in fact very much astonished to learn from
Madame de Guigné that the elder little girl, who
had struck her as being such an exceptionally
sweet, gentle child, had been most troublesome and
difficult to manage only a few months before.

"I first took charge of Anne when she was four
and a half years of age," writes Mlle. B., "and I was
really charmed by the easy grace of her manner as
she came to greet me. One could not help loving
her. Although so tiny, there was something about
her even then that inspired respect. She was very
sensible too, and she had such a kind little
heart. . . . When we returned to the Chateau at
Annecy, she was very anxious about me for fear I
should fret over leaving my parents who lived near
Cannes. Almost as soon as we arrived, she took
me around the garden and wanted me to pick some
flowers. 'You must do just as if this was your own
home,' she said; 'pick all the flowers you like and
send them to your mother to comfort her.' The
next morning I heard a soft little knock at my door.
It was the dear child coming to see if I had slept
well! All day long she was trying to help me. . . .
and when we went for a walk she would let the
others go with their mother while she took my
hand, for fear, as she said, that 'Demoise might feel
left out.' Anne was always so sweet and unselfish."
Rather different from the little lady who would not

have anyone else sit on her mother's lap!

"Demoise" was the quaint name Anne had invented for the governess. And why? The reason is illuminating: "I'm going to call her that," she explained, "because 'Mademoiselle' sounds so stiff, and we want to make her feel at home." There was always a wonderful delicacy in her courtesy.

Of course Anne came of a great race. Madame de Guigné traces her descent not only from St. Louis of France, "the perfect knight," but also from General de Charette, who fought for the Pope with the Pontifical Zouaves. After the Italian campaign, the Frenchmen returned to support their own country in the Franco-Prussian war. It was then, during the retreat of the French troops at the battle of Patay, that de Charette raised the banner of the Sacred Heart and led his heroic little band, three hundred strong, against two thousand Prussians.

But in Anne there was more than the courtesy of kings or a soldier's courage. She had that which made St. Louis a perfect knight: the charity of God which "is patient. . . . that dealeth not perversely, seeketh not her own. . . . beareth all things, hopeth all things, endureth all things."

Chapter 2

THE GREAT MEETING

AS EARLY as June 1915, when she was only four and a half, Anne had spoken of her First Communion. She had always loved Our Lord, though at first, like most of us, she loved herself as well; but since the great day when she turned her whole heart to God, the desire to possess Him in Holy Communion became stronger and stronger.

That autumn, when the family went to their house in Cannes for the winter, her mother thought Anne was old enough to join the catechism class at the Auxiliatrice convent. This was an immense joy to the little one, for she felt she was now preparing for the great event in real earnest, though she knew she was a good deal younger than most first communicants.

To her, catechism was not just "a lesson." She really cared about it. Most children want to find out everything about the people or things they are interested in. Anne's interest was in Our Lord. She really loved Him, so she wanted to find out all about Him and the things He taught.

At that time the catechism class was taught by Mother St. Raymond, a most holy nun and a very good judge of child nature by reason of her naturally keen insight and long experience. She very quickly saw that the little newcomer, though only five years old, was far ahead of all the rest in something more than brains.

"I soon saw," she once said, "that Anne was a very gifted child; but what struck me most was this: the others were never jealous of her, though she was cleverer than any of them and the youngest. This is a remarkable thing, but it is true. Every one of them loved and admired her. I think it was because she never tried to 'show off' or get the better of anyone. Her manner was so sweet too. She always seemed to know how to adapt herself to other people's tastes, and she was as nice with some rather spoiled children as with those who behaved well. I do not think I ever saw her in a bad humor or upset over anything.

"At first she had a little difficulty in learning by heart, so one day I told her to repeat in her own words all she had understood of the day's lesson. It was about the Church, a difficult subject for a small child, and I did not expect much; but to my great surprise she had understood it all and repeated the whole lesson in astonishingly clear and precise words. It often seemed as if God must have taught her."

Once a priest asked Anne where the Holy Spirit dwelt specially. "In the souls of the just," came the quick answer. Now no one remembered teaching her that. It is of course quite possible that she had heard it in some sermon, but the frequency of such answers makes it impossible to deny that she must have had an understanding of spiritual things which was, to say the least, unusual in a child of five.

"She listened eagerly to all I said," Mother St. Raymond continues, "but she never tried to answer out of her turn, or in fact until she was questioned; but very often all heads would turn in her direction when nobody knew the lesson—and they were not mistaken. 'This little girl knows everything!' a nine-year-old once said. And she answered so sweetly too, in her dear little voice (she had such a tiny whisper of a voice you could hardly hear it), but what energy there was in her and what courage! It was such a contrast."

When she began to prepare Anne for her first Confession, Mother St. Raymond was again surprised, for she found that the child not only knew her faults, but analyzed them with a judgment as correct as it was careful. Not that Anne was scrupulous—there was never a sign of foolish scrupulosity in her either then or later—but she made her examination of conscience with a gravity and care that impressed all those who had to deal with her. Nor was she frightened about her first Confession. "Afraid of the priest!" she said to Mother St. Raymond, looking up at her with innocent amazement. "Why should I be? You said he would be acting as Our Lord!"

Anne loved God and she also knew what even the smallest imperfection meant to God. Love is a wonderful searchlight when it plays upon the conscience of a soul. No one who loved God as Anne did could ever feel sure she had loved Him per-

fectly, still less could she feel sure that she had
loved her neighbor with anything like perfection.
She knew well enough that we often irritate or dis-
appoint people and so cause them to sin.

There was Melanie the cook, for instance, a good
woman, but one whose tongue was not so golden
as her heart. "Dear Lord, what can I *possibly* have
done to Melanie?" her governess heard Anne praying one day when the cook had sent her off with
some tart remark. Melanie knows now what her
sharp word meant to the dear child that she loved
indeed with all her warm old heart, but whom she
had pierced with one of the little thorns of her
tongue. What would she not give today to be able
to unsay that sharp word!

Perhaps Anne was sensitive, but she had learned
the lesson of sensitivity. She never pricked anyone.
She would keep no "little thorns under *her* tongue."[1]

"Not only did I never hear her say an unkind
word," says Mother St. Raymond, "but she never
even teased the other children, and this must have
meant considerable self-control, for she was naturally so quick and sharp."

And so the winter months went by, and it was
perfectly evident to Madame de Guigné and to the
nuns that Anne was fully prepared to make her
First Communion. Her confessor too was of the
same opinion, but the Bishop made difficulties
when he saw the name of a child of five on the
list of first communicants. However, when it was

1. From Kipling's *Jungle Books*.

presented to him again that Anne was by far the most intelligent child in the class, His Excellency finally agreed to give his consent, but only on condition that the little girl should be put through a rigorous examination by no less a person than the Superior of the Jesuits, who was by no means disposed in her favor. In fact, when he saw how extremely small she was,[2] he remarked: "Really, it is rather absurd to present such a baby. The mothers will soon want them to make their First Communion before they can walk!"

The interview seemed likely to be rather a terrible ordeal and her mother trembled for the result; but Anne went into the Father's room quite unconcerned. She wanted Our Lord and she was sure she could make even a severe examiner understand that, so she did not worry. Besides, though she never put herself forward at school, it was out of humility, not shyness. She was still the born leader when there was anything to be done. The retirement Mother St. Raymond speaks of was simply the delicacy of true humility that will not "show off."

Of strangers she certainly had no fear, for the story goes that about this very time a gentleman called to see her mother, who happened to be out. But his business was important, so he decided to await Madame de Guigné's return. Anne, however, was at home and she gravely walked into the room and talked with him politely till her mother arrived. "Visitors are very tiresome, aren't they, Mother?"

---

2. Just then Anne was small even for her age.

the blasé little hostess remarked afterwards. "But I thought he might find it dull to wait alone so I went down and entertained him." The gentleman had been very much entertained.

But to return to the examination. The learned Jesuit did not keep to the order of the catechism, but questioned Anne up and down at random in a way that would have upset any child who did not really know the subject; but he was quickly convinced that she was perfectly prepared. He became so interested in her, moreover, that he prolonged the interview for some time, questioning her on all sorts of subjects and even probing the little one's conscience.

"What is your chief fault?" he asked.

"Pride," answered Anne promptly, "and disobedience too."

"Humility here," thought the priest, but he pretended to be very stern and told her that a little girl who wanted to receive Our Lord must obey at once and do whatever she was told. Then with a quick turn he asked: "When does Jesus obey?"

"At Mass," answered the child without any hesitation.

"What words does He obey?"

"He obeys the priest when he says: 'This is My Body, this is My Blood.'"

Then the examiner tried another subject.

"What Sacraments have you received?"

"Baptism and Penance," she replied.

"And which are you hoping to receive?"

"The Holy Eucharist and Confirmation."

"No more?"

"Perhaps some day I shall receive the Sacrament of Matrimony," she suggested.

"Holy Orders too, eh?"

"Oh no, Father, how could I? That's *your* Sacrament!" The little maid was not to be caught tripping.

Outside, Mother St. Raymond was getting more and more anxious, but at length they both appeared smiling, to her great relief. "I wish you and I were as well prepared to receive Our Lord as this little girl is," was the examiner's verdict.

All obstacles being now removed, Anne joined the first communicants' retreat at the convent. It was given by one of the Jesuits who took for his text: "Obedience is the sanctity of children." All those little ones listened with good will no doubt, but as in Our Lord's time, "the seeds fell, some on thorny ground, some by the wayside and some on good ground."

For Anne the Father's words were a revelation. Being a saint, then, for a little girl, meant being obedient. Being obedient meant pleasing Jesus; and as she wanted to please Jesus, she must therefore be obedient. The logical little mind had put the matter with a clarity worthy of St. Thomas. All that remained was to carry it out; and with Anne, to know was to act, so it was done. From that time forth she was practically perfect in obedience.

At last the great day came. Anne was radiant when she arrived at the convent, but soon Mother St. Raymond saw a sad look on her face.

"What is it, dear?" she asked.

"Daddy is not here," said the child.

"But he is with Our Lord," answered the nun, "and so he is much closer to you than if he stood beside you."

"Oh," said Anne, drinking in the great truth. "Oh, then I'm quite, *quite* happy."

It was the 26th of March, 1917, and Monday in Passion week. A strange day for the First Communion of a little child, but that year it was also the feast of Our Lady's Annunciation, transferred one day, because the 25th fell on Passion Sunday. And so it was under the shadow of the purple that His Mother brought Jesus this little white soul who later on, when she had learned to write a bit, laboriously traced these words as her First Communion resolution: "I will give my sacrifices to Mary, so that she may give them to Jesus."

Anne never spoke of this first great Meeting, but those who saw her were struck by her wonderful expression. "It is impressed on my mind forever," says Mother St. Raymond. "Later in the day I was speaking to the group of first communicants and said to them: 'Now we have given you the very best gift we could, for we have allowed you to receive Jesus.' At these words Anne's eyes flashed with a joy that I shall never forget. She said something I could not hear, but her expression was so beautiful. I always felt that what we saw of her life was a mere nothing, the real beauty was within."

Anne at age two and a half.

Anne (right) and Marinette (left) with their dog "Rajah."

Upper: Prayer written by Anne; and page from a notebook in which she recorded her sacrifices for Jesus each day. The prayer says: "O my dear little Jesus, I love You."
Lower: Anne's little book of prayers before and after Holy Communion.

Chapel of St. Gertrude, where Anne made her First Communion. This is the convent chapel of the Auxiliatrice Nuns, called in England the Helpers of the Holy Souls.

Anne and "The Others": Jojo (top left), Anne (top right),
Marinette (lower left), and Lelaine (lower right).

Anne's home: Château de la Cour, near Annecy-le-Vieux (Old Annecy). The Chateau overlooks the Lake of Annecy.

The Lake of Annecy

A famous photograph of Anne.

Anne toward the end of her life.

The room where Anne died (in the family's winter home in Cannes).

Chapter 3

"THE PROOF OF LOVE IS WORK."

Probatio dilectionis exhibitio est operis.
—St. Gregory

THE love that had been lit up in Anne's heart at the first great Meeting was to grow and grow till it filled all her life.

At first she could hardly believe it was true that her Lord had really come into her heart at last, and very often during the day, when the thought of it came back to her mind, she would stop playing to squeeze her hands together and whisper: "Oh, *thank you*, Jesus." It was just a little burst of gratitude that could not be suppressed. Once too, Mlle. B. found her kneeling in a corner, evidently praying, and when she questioned her, Anne said: "I was only thanking Jesus for being so kind as to come into my heart."

These visits of Our Lord were the great joy of her life and colored her thoughts so much that she used to think everyone felt the same. "Jojo, remember you are going to Holy Communion tomorrow," she would say to her little brother when all other entreaties had failed to make him be good. To her this was the most powerful motive of all. She simply could not believe anyone would refuse to be touched by it. And she was seldom wrong, for her own earnestness usually carried others along with her.

Anne had always been particularly anxious to carry Jojo with her in all that she cared most about, so he was naturally the one to whom she poured out her feelings about the visits that meant so much to her. But he was still very small and little boys' souls often wake up rather slowly, so she did not always find him as sympathetic as she expected. He could not yet quite understand what Nenette was so excited about. After all, he was only four when she made her First Communion, so it was really not very surprising that he did not warm up much when she would tell him how wonderful it was to receive Holy Communion. "Oh, wait till you have been, Jojo," the disappointed little sister would cry; "you don't know what you are talking about. You can't imagine how lovely it is."

But if Jojo was unsympathetic, there were others who understood: her mother, Mademoiselle, and Mother St. Raymond. Her aunt, too, Mother St. Joseph, who was Superioress of the convent. All these had felt the joy which was so new and beautiful to her. She knew they understood, and she smiled at them, but she did not speak much of the great Meetings. What Our Lord said to her was the "secret of the King."

Mother St. Raymond suspected, however, that this child's relations with Our Lord were more than ordinary, and one day she succeeded in raising the veil a little. She knew Anne looked up to the nuns

with a reverence almost like that which she showed
to priests, because she realized that they too were
consecrated to the service of God. Even at her First
Confession, she went to the priest without fear,
telling him everything "because he holds the place
of Our Lord," and in her simplicity she was ready
to extend some of this confidence to the nuns. She
knew of course that they did not hold the great
office of the priesthood, but she felt they were close
to Our Lord somehow, and so she reverenced them.
"You can tell anything to the nuns, you know," she
was often heard saying to her little sisters. And so
when Mother St. Raymond asked her casually one
day if Our Lord ever said anything to her, though
she hesitated for a moment, evidently unwilling to
break her reserve, yet she answered simply:

"Not always, but sometimes when I am very
quiet."

"What does He say?" continued the nun.

Anne hesitated again, then she looked up with
that wonderful expression and said softly:

"He tells me that He loves me."

Another time it was her aunt, Mother St. Joseph,
who drew out a little more of the beautiful secret.

"Jesus says He loves me," the child confided to
her. "He says He loves me much more than I love
Him!"

But Anne too had plenty to say. She told her
mother one day how much better she could pray
without a book. "You see," she explained, "if I use
my book I get distracted; but I don't if I just talk
to Jesus, because I always know what to say when

I talk to people."

"What do you say to Him?" asked her mother.

"I tell Him I love Him," Anne answered simply, with that look which said so much.

Evidently, Jesus and Anne were friends.[1]

*   *   *

But joy such as that can be bought only at a great price. Our Lord had said: "If you love Me, keep My Commandments. . . and I will come unto you and your heart shall rejoice and your joy no man shall take from you."

"Obedience is the sanctity of children," Anne had been told during her first retreat, and she knew what it meant. First, obedience to the first great Commandment: "Thou shalt love the Lord thy God with thy whole heart"; then obedience to the second, which is like to the first, but generally much harder: "Thou shalt love thy neighbor as thyself"; and finally, obedience to all the rest, which, for a little child, is usually sufficiently fulfilled by doing whatever she is told.

There is not so much need to dwell specially on Anne's love of God, for it is plainly evident in

----

1. Here is a little story that cannot be left out: On the eve of Corpus Christi, when she was about six years old, Anne happened to see one of the nuns at Annecy arranging flowers for the altar. Anne came close and watched her for a moment, then she said: "Sister, I would so like to make a bouquet for Jesus. May I help you?" The permission granted, she set to work very gravely, picking out the most beautiful flowers she could find for her bunch. Then with shining eyes she brought it to the nun, saying: "Will you put it very close to Him, please?"

every story told about her. It was both the magnet that drew her on and her "reward exceeding great." But her obedience to the second great Commandment must be studied in some detail, for it is a great example of that fidelity in the fiery test of daily life which can only be found in the way of sacrifice.

"I have never known Anne to refuse a sacrifice." This is Mlle. B.'s carefully considered statement; and she had lived with Anne from the year 1916, when she was only four years old, till her death in 1922 at the age of eleven. Only a few times in her early years was the little girl known to have shown hesitation over an act of obedience or a sacrifice, though sometimes there would be a little sign of the hard struggle that victory cost her. Usually the first word of reproof was sufficient to cure her of a fault, but there were times, especially at first, when she had to be reminded more often.

One word had stopped her putting both hands into the basket of blessed bread in church,[2] but many reminders were needed to cure her tiresome habit of continually bending down to pull up her socks when she was out for a walk.

"Don't do that, Nenette," Mlle. B. would say.

"Oh, I'm sorry," the little girl answered quickly

---

2. In France, ordinary bread is blessed and distributed during Mass on Sundays. It has no connection with the Holy Eucharist, but is a survival of the ancient custom of the Church when the faithful brought bread and wine for the Sacrifice, and whatever was not needed used to be distributed to the poor afterwards.

and walked along properly for a few yards. But very soon, down she would go again, fidgeting with her socks as usual.

"Don't, dear."

"Oh, I *am* so sorry."

Then the little back straightened firmly and next time the impulse to bend down was checked halfway. She would forget again perhaps, but all her will was set on obedience, so she soon got control of the instinct and no more reminders were necessary.

Is this a trifle? Let those who think it a trifle try to give up some tiny instinctive habit of their own.

As Jesus stood one day in the Temple He saw a "certain poor widow casting two brass mites into the treasury. And He said: 'Verily I say to you that this poor woman hath cast in more than the rest. . . for she hath given all she had.'"

This was Anne's greatness. She was only a baby with a baby's sacrifices to make, but *they were all she had.* God "looketh not to the gift, but to the love of the giver."

When she was about seven Anne lost her first tooth. This was an event that all four children had been awaiting with much excitement, because someone had told them that when anybody lost their first tooth a present was sure to arrive. So Anne, minus a tooth, rushed to tell the great news, followed by the others all wild with excitement. When would the present come? Where would it come from? Who would send it?

No grown-up vouchsafed any satisfactory answer, but a big parcel did arrive that afternoon addressed to Anne. It contained a wonderful dolls' washstand which ran real water. Of course she was in ecstasy over it and all four were soon playing happily.

However, one of them was a little boy. No one quite knew how he did it, but suddenly the beautiful china toy was on the ground in pieces. For a moment Anne stared in stunned silence, then she turned and saw that Jojo was crying. He loved his sister and he had not meant to break it. Immediately Anne's arms were around him, her own trouble pushed into the background while she comforted him. Afterwards when the others had run off to play again, she looked at the pieces of her treasure and then, smiling through the tears that would come, she said: "I'm glad, because now I have made Abraham's sacrifice."

It was a big thing to say. Was she right? Who shall judge her? In the matter of the sacrifice there was a vast difference in all truth. Of Abraham God asked the life of his only son; Anne's holocaust was a broken toy, but it was her *treasure*. God wanted it and she gave it. There is the simple fact.

Perhaps it was her deep insight into the spirit of sacrifice which made Anne understand Our Lady so well. Certain it is that as she grew older she began to love her best at the foot of the Cross. The Mother of Sorrows for her was "Our Lady of Consolation," and this was the title she gave to a little statue in the garden which was near at hand when the children were playing. Here she could turn for help when the struggle for self-control became very hard. It was in the midst of a game, in fact, that she first thought of the name, and as usual she passed on her idea to the others: "We must go to Our Lady for comfort when things go wrong."

Anne drew a picture too about the same time— a very quaint, angular picture, but evidently intended to represent Our Lady—and she wrote underneath it: "At the foot of the Cross to which her Son was nailed, Mary wept. Give me the grace to weep with thee." And when they asked her why she wished to weep, she answered: "Because Jesus is not loved enough." It was Our Lady's own reason.

Jesus was teaching the little one great lessons now that He was Master of her heart. Not that the way of the Cross was entirely new to Anne, for her mother had begun very early to train her child to deny herself, and the baby would sometimes listen and try to offer some little thing "that Daddy may come back to us safe." But later, when his death had opened her eyes to the great truths of life, it came so willingly. "For France, dear," her mother would say when something unpleasant had to be done, and Anne obeyed.

A sharp taste of suffering came to try her not long after her father's death. She got a rather bad case of influenza, and various painful things had to be done. Mustard poultices, for instance, were put on her chest, which is not a pleasant process; but the child bore it bravely, and if an involuntary cry escaped her, it was immediately crushed by the prayer that had become a habit: "Jesus, I offer it to You."

Soon after, God tried her patience on another side. It was paratyphoid this time, an illness which means months of tiresome dieting after the worst has passed. Anne could soon get up and play again, but the dull regime of milk and tasteless soups went on for a long time. Yet she would eat her dreary dinner without complaint, whatever interesting things the others might be having. And Anne liked nice things.

In her unconverted days she had been known to steal some sweets that had been put well out of her reach—so her mother thought. They were on top of a high cupboard in fact, but, as St. Vincent de Paul said in a better cause: "Difficulties only exist to be overcome." Anne certainly thought so, and as soon as her mother's attention was diverted for a moment, she collected chairs and stools and finally clambered up till she was high enough to reach the box of sweets. So her patience now over milk pudding was not indifference, but obedience. Very blind obedience too, it must have been, for small children are not much impressed by medical reasons for a tiresome diet.

As she grew older, Anne went much further than this. Not only did she take unpleasant things that were ordered, but when the children came down to dessert, she often refrained from some of the nice things that were there for her to take and she never reminded anyone if she was passed over when sweets were handed round.[3] She was, in fact, rather clever at managing to get herself forgotten. Her face would light up with pleasure, Mlle. B. relates, when she found she had been overlooked when something delicious was being given. As she grew older she generally managed it by being very busy looking after the others. Anne was always such a little mother that her self-denial frequently went unnoticed, but occasionally she was caught.

One day the children were promised a great treat. They were to have some very special Brittany pancakes which had to be eaten hot, just as they came from the pan. All four sat watching the frying pan in great excitement, and when the first pancake was served, hot, crisp and golden, Jojo had it of course. Leleine got the next, and then came baby Marinette's turn. Anne had been very busy running to and fro getting plates and seeing that all the little party were served. Now each child had had one and the second round began with undiminished appetites. Suddenly the nurse realized that Anne had not even sat down yet. She had had no pancakes at all and there she was giving all the others a second helping. "Why Miss Anne," she exclaimed, "what about you? I don't believe you have had one at all yet, have you?" Anne got pink and laughed; she was well caught this time, so she sat down at once and had her share.

---

3. It is worth remarking that Anne took the plain things that were good for her and left the pleasant extras, such as candied fruits and sweets which were given for dessert.

Another day there was a picnic in prospect. It was to be a long outing, and when the day came, the weather was perfect; but little Marinette was not well. She could not go; but must she fret all alone with no one to play with? Anne could not bear to think of it, so she offered to stay and keep Marinette company.

Next time it was Jojo who was sick when there was to be a party. This time the prospect was more enticing for her than for him, since the little girls were planning to have a dolls' dinner, but Anne had made up her mind to stay at home with her brother and she kept to her resolution, though she was sorely tempted. She stood at the door and looked a little "down" as she watched the happy party setting off, but she soon conquered her feelings and ran back to amuse Jojo.

There was indeed nothing Anne would not do for "the others," as she called them. From the time she was four she had carried them all in her heart with more than a mother's love, for it was their souls she loved most. "I don't care what they do to me, as long as they are good," she often said, and sometimes they did a good deal. They were dear children on the whole and very fond of her, but small boys and girls are not naturally thoughtful, and Anne had so completely hidden her own likes and dislikes that they soon forgot she had any. Opportunities for self-denial, therefore, were not wanting.

Anne still instinctively took the initiative whenever there was anything to be done, but her powers were now only used to help others in any way she could. At games and on all the little occasions when selfishness is so natural, she invariably did what the others wanted. Over and over again she would play the games she did not like, or take the part that was not popular, or go on when she was tired and wanted to stop. The others expected it of her, for they had never known her unwilling and it did not occur to them that Anne could mind things. Never did they guess their sweet little sister was an imperious little tyrant inside. They were too young to remember her early days, but their mother had not forgotten, nor had Mademoiselle.

Sometimes at first Anne had been almost overcome by the struggle for self-control. She would leave the game and rush up to Mlle. B. with flaming cheeks and tears in her eyes, gasping out: "Oh, how I do *want* to be cross!" Then after a moment, she got hold of her feelings, the tears would be swallowed and she would run back to the others, smiling happily as if nothing was the matter. This happened occasionally, but most often only God saw the struggle in its fierceness; Mademoiselle, even with her sharp eyes, could scarcely catch a glimpse of it, so well did the child hide her pain.

Even her treasures Anne would willingly give up if she thought anyone else wanted them. There was a certain wheelbarrow she was very fond of, partly because her father had given it to her and also because, well—it just suited her. But it also just suited Jojo and so he too often wanted it—usually, of course, when he saw her playing with it. But she let him have it, and a smile too, generally.

Once, however, Anne found it hard work to produce the smile. She had been arranging some flowers in her little barrow and had just succeeded in making what she thought was a wonderful show, when Jojo and another little boy came along, threw out her precious flowers, seized the barrow without a word and ran off with it. For a moment it was too much for Anne, but she crushed the quickly rising temper and smiling bravely up at Mademoiselle: "It's all right," she gulped. "I don't mind if they want it."

About this very time in another part of France, a little boy[4] who is also a candidate for the honors of the Church made a very profound remark to his mother: "'Yes' is the nicest word we can say to Jesus." The whole secret of sanctity is in that sentence.

Anne said "Yes" to Jesus very often, so often that her whole life was one big "Yes" to all Our Lord asked of her.

She said "Yes" in every detail of life, till even the actual word became such an instinct that when her mother bent over the bed to kiss her goodnight, she would still sleepily murmur: "Yes, Mamma."

If she went to sleep with "Yes" on her lips, she woke with it too. There was never any need to call Anne twice. The others, as usual, took her perfection for granted.

_____

4. Guy de Fontgalland (died 1925, aged 12).

"Nurse had hard work to get us up this morning," one of her sisters said the day after they had been on a picnic. "We all needed plenty of calls, except Nenette. But of course she always gets up at once."

Anne was often a great help to Nurse by her tact in keeping the peace between these two little girls, who were rather different in character and inclined to quarrel if left to themselves, which naturally somewhat hindered the getting dressed process.

She did not spend much time at the mirror either. Once when she was about four, and only just "converted," Mlle. B. found her standing on a chair surveying her reflection in a mirror with some satisfaction. "I'm rather pretty, don't you think so?" she remarked innocently.

Mademoiselle replied that little girls should not waste their time looking at the mirror, and anyhow, no matter how pretty one may be, beauty is a gift of God and we should not be vain over it.

Somewhat abashed by this answer, Anne jumped off the chair and never again was heard to praise herself, nor did she seem to care how she looked, though she was always careful enough to be tidy. She was not hurt some years later when a friend remarked that her second teeth were not so nice as the first ones had been. "Jesus likes them well enough," was all she answered.

"Anne was really mortified in all her senses," says Mother St. Raymond. "She had an instinctive horror of anything that was not absolutely pure. 'I want my heart to be as pure as a lily for Jesus.' This was her First Communion prayer, and she was just *that*. It struck everyone. 'She has such pure eyes,' some-one said to me once. She had indeed, and she used them purely.

"I had told the children to be careful not to look at anything unpleasant in the streets or elsewhere, and I am sure she obeyed me most strictly, for she seemed to have great control over her eyes. Even at the catechism class she looked only at me and did not give way to that curiosity which is so nat-ural to children. Nor did she ask for anything she fancied. When I brought something to show them, Anne never rushed forward to see what it was; she would wait till the others had seen as much as they wanted, or till I called her to come and look."

In church she thought only of God and looked only at Him. Very many people were struck by the beautiful way she behaved there.

Another day when Anne was in church, a woman without faith came into the house of God. She had not meant to pray, but she saw one who loved Him and she was conquered. "Never again," she declared afterwards, "no, never again, will I say there is no God."

It was not that Anne ever put on a pious air or did anything extraordinary. On the contrary, she knelt beside her mother, like any other little girl, absolutely simple and natural, but looked at the altar with such adoring love that the most thought-less were awed in spite of themselves.

At first she followed the Mass in a picture prayer

book, but when she could read she would join in the prayers of the Church, for she loved the Liturgy. When the Canon of the Mass began, however, she would shut her eyes and unite herself to Our Lord in her own way. She kept very still during these solemn moments, but when it was time to go up to the altar her face shone with joy and she went forward eagerly. Those who have seen Anne receive Holy Communion, will never forget the sight. "She looked like a living monstrance," one person declared, "her face was radiant." Absolutely absorbed in Our Lord, joy filled her whole being to the exclusion of everything else, so it is only natural that something of it shone through.

It is rather curious that this little twentieth-century child should have been led by her love of God to do the very same thing as the great pioneers of the Liturgy did in those early days when Christianity was young. She composed a canticle to be sung at the time of Holy Communion. It was a very simple little song, quite innocent of rhyme or measure, yet prompted by the same spirit which inspired her great forefathers in the Faith. It has not the majesty of that ancient Gaulish canticle: "*Venite populi, ad sacrum et immortale mysterium,*" sung for so many ages by the people of France; but childish though Anne's little song may be, it was the instinct of the ages of faith that made her write it. She would like to go singing to meet her God:

> O Mary, my dear Mother,
> Lend me thy Son for one short moment.
> Lay Him in my humble arms.

O Mary, let me kiss the feet of thy dear Son,
He has given me so many graces.
O Mary, how I want to receive thy Son in my arms,
Give Him to me, please give Him to me!

Then returning from the altar:

Now how happy I am
For I have Him with me.

And the pathetic little refrain that was the cry
of her heart all day long:

O Mary, give Him to me, please give Him to me,
I want your Son, please give Him to me!

Chapter 4

THE APOSTLE OF THE NURSERY

NOW that she had wholly turned to God, the strength in Anne's character which had made her such a little tyrant in her babyhood began to be used to great purpose in the cause of God. She now loved God so intensely that she felt she could not do enough to show her love.

"Nothing costs much when we love Him," she said to a little friend. That was how she felt, and she was so full of her new idea that she did not realize that others might not feel the same. Only experience can teach patience.

Since she understood so clearly that the highest happiness on earth is to serve God perfectly, she naturally wanted those she loved to have this greatest of joys, so she began to try and persuade her brother and sisters to join in the race for perfection. Accustomed as they were to follow their beloved leader, the three children went some way up the steep path, but being only ordinary little mortals, they could not keep her pace and sometimes, very much out of breath, they sat down!

"Oh, bother! Look here, Nenette, you do it today and I'll do it tomorrow!" Jojo burst out one day at dessert. Anne had been telling him that he ought to deny himself sometimes, when there were so *many* delicious things.

She probably did do it that day and many other days as well, for the Apostle of the nursery was not one to preach what she did not practice. And being a very practical little soul, she made her self-denial "profit the poor," as St. John Chrysostom advised, for the goodies which she did not eat usually found their way to the maids or were taken to poor people she knew in the village.

Once, Anne's ingenuity devised a very profitable use for the results of their "economy" at table and one that fired the enthusiasm of her disciples. There had been a fire in the village and one poor woman with four small children was homeless. Anne was very much distressed when she heard about it. She felt she must help somehow, but there seemed nothing a little girl could do. At last a brilliant idea came into her head. They would have a bazaar, she and Jojo and the two little ones; then they would give the proceeds to the poor homeless mother!

At first it was a great secret, not even Mademoiselle was told, and they all valiantly saved sweets and various other treasures, while Anne became extremely busy making the sort of things that she thought people bought at bazaars. She really had very clever fingers, so quite a number of handcrafted items were soon collected in the secret hiding place where the committee brought their contributions. Finally, when they thought there was enough, Anne solemnly asked her mother's per-

mission to have a bazaar and invited everyone to
come to it with full purses.

It really was a bazaar worth going to! Stalls were
arranged under the trees in the garden, and very
remarkable stalls they were too. The first thing visitors came to was that most popular place, the
refreshment buffet, well stocked with sweets, candied fruit and little cakes. They were sold at a good
price, but they had been bought at a greater one,
for everything there had been saved by the brave
children from their own dessert. Dishes of fruit were
there too; blackberries, nuts and other things that
they had found in the woods, all nicely arranged
to tempt the guests.

On the right stood a flower stall where daisies,
dandelions and various wild flowers were selling at
huge prices. But best of all was Anne's own special effort, the handicraft stall. This was laden with
a wonderful array of curious little articles. There
were tiny cradles scooped out of acorns, baskets
carved from horse chestnuts, bags woven with
rushes and other homemade things, all done by
Anne's clever fingers. The visitors were enthusias-
tic and a brisk sale went on till all the stalls were
cleared and the enormous sum of thirty francs
rewarded the delighted little organizer for her toil—
not at all a bad sum for a little girl of eight to
have earned all by herself. It is easy to imagine her
delight at being able to give such really substan-
tial help to the poor woman, who was touched
indeed when she heard that the child had not
merely asked her mother for the money, but had

worked so hard to obtain it. This was charity worthy of the name.

Mother St. Raymond has a somewhat similar story which is worth telling, because it proves once again that Anne's charity was very real.

"I had told the children," she says, "that we were going to work for the poor. There would be an auction and the bidding must be with sacrifices. "Whoever makes the most sacrifices," I said, "will be able to buy the most toys for the poor children at Christmas." So they all tried hard and before Christmas we had the auction. I kept the best item—a beautiful doll—for the end. They began to bid for it, higher and higher till their collections were exhausted. All but Anne's, for she outbid everyone and the doll fell to her. I think she paid for it with more than a hundred sacrifices."[1]

Another time when Anne's charitable ideas succeeded in arousing her brother and sisters was the day when they found that the rabbits had died at the convent in Annecy. The children were all much distressed, but Anne's kind heart was at once stirred to action. As soon as they got home she called a council and the four unanimously agreed to ask leave to open their money boxes and buy the poor nuns some more rabbits. To their great joy they found that there was enough to get two bunnies,

---

1. It should be clearly understood that there was no incentive to pride in this. No one knew what another's sacrifices were. It was merely a way of teaching them to deny themselves for the sake of others. It was rather like the

so the next day a proud and happy party went to purchase the pair and then carried them in triumph to the convent. But Anne's charity did not end there. After considering the matter, she had come to the conclusion that the nuns evidently did not know what rabbits really liked to eat, so she asked the Sister about it. "You know," she said, "what they like best of all are sow thistles." As the Sister did not seem quite sure what these were, the four children went off and picked some. Then, having left the bunnies with a good supply, they ran home, hoping these two would thrive better than the last.

At Réray where they used to stay sometimes, there was an old woman called Jeanne who helped in the kitchen. Now one day Anne happened to see Jeanne in the yard plucking fowls. She went up to her, of course, for she always wanted to help anyone who seemed busy. At this particular moment, however, the old woman was not exactly working but hunting, for the chickens' feathers were rather thickly populated with fleas and poor Jeanne was engaged in trying to catch what she could of those which had migrated onto herself. Anne

---

"Crib straw" collected in some schools. At the beginning of Advent a pile of straw is placed in a quiet corner where people can go unobserved. Each one who has made some act of self-denial or charity may take a straw from the first heap and place it on one side to form another, but you are not supposed to let anyone see you do this. On Christmas Eve the second heap is placed in the Crib, so that the Infant Jesus rests on straw that has been bought at a price.

quickly saw what was the matter and she joined in the chase! "You mustn't be the only one to suffer, Jeanne," she said. "I'll have half." And she spent a long time trying to catch the fleas before they hopped, so that the old woman could go on peacefully plucking.

Anne loved all those who worked for her. Even on her deathbed she insisted on choosing some little Christmas presents for the maids, though the least movement caused her such terrible pain that she could not hold anything. She wanted them to know that she had not forgotten them. Not that they needed any reminders, for she had always been so sweet to everyone in the house.

Anne had a respect for workers and, strange to say, a great sympathy for the poor, for though brought up in the midst of wealth, she had somehow realized what it meant to be in want. When quite a small child she asked her mother one day how the poor people managed to keep warm in winter, because she had heard someone say they would have nothing for their fires that year. Madame de Guigné then told her little daughter the sad truth that many poor people do *not* manage to keep warm, but suffer very much from cold. It was a revelation to the child, and she began to cry. Her tender little heart was hurt to think that there was suffering in the world which she could not prevent. But her tears soon dried, for her mother suggested that she should learn to make some warm clothes which would comfort at least a few poor folk. Anne was delighted and set to work at once on some simple knitting with such energy that she was soon able to make scarves and other little things.

A real labor of love it was, for she would not be satisfied unless the things were well done, no matter how many times she had to undo her work. "It must be well done if it is for the poor children," she used to say, for she had not forgotten that Our Lord said: "What you do to the least of My little ones, you do to Me." That is why, when her mother made up a parcel for the poor, Anne used to choose some of her nicest dolls and toys for them, not the old broken ones.

But there was one thing Anne loved more than helping the poor, and that was helping *souls*, especially poor souls, those that were cold in love and starved of God's grace—starved through their own fault, no doubt, but no less pathetic for that.

Anne's intense love of God made her dread sin as a terrible evil to be avoided at all costs, but it also taught her, as it teaches all the Saints, to love the sinner and to help him. Even as a little child she had begun to realize what sin meant to Our Lord and how it made Him suffer, but as she grew older it hurt her more keenly than anything that affected herself. She felt it must be prevented somehow, people must be brought back to Our Lord and taught to love Him. She wanted to go and do it herself, to teach people about God and make them understand how He loved them, to touch their hearts and persuade them to be good as she had done with Jojo.

But a little girl cannot go out "into the high-ways and hedges and compel them to come in." How she wished she could! But Anne was always practical, and so she threw her energy into what she had the power to do, that is, to win them by prayer. And this, after all, is the first part of an apostle's work, for if he does not pray before he preaches he will never lead souls to God. So Anne prayed, in the true sense of the word—that is to say, she prayed not only with her lips and her heart, but with her life. All the actions of her day, little and great, pleasant and painful, went up as the smoke of incense before the throne of God.

She was His, and her works were His, for she had given Him her heart and her will to use for His own glory. Could He refuse her? One would think not, but Anne added more than the ordinary round of daily duty when she wanted grace for some soul whom she knew to be in danger. "Nothing would stop her," writes Madame de Guigné, "when she meant to save a soul. She would sacrifice her-self in countless little ways and never lost a chance of offering something to God for her poor sinner."

Of course, Anne was too young to know much of the evil that exists in the world, but she knew it did exist and that the nuns often came into con-tact with these wicked people, so she used to ask them to give her a soul to convert, a really big sin-ner, preferably. She would listen very gravely till she knew all about her sinner, then with a most businesslike air, she would say firmly: "I will see about it," as though she had an understanding with

Our Lord on the matter.

Nothing discouraged the little apostle. If the sinner was obdurate, she prayed the harder and enlisted the whole family in a crusade of prayer. Resistance roused her zeal and she urged everyone to persevere till they had wrenched the grace from God. "We must go on praying, Mother," she said when she heard that an obstinate old man, whose heart was as hard as the mountains amidst which he lived, still persisted in refusing the Sacraments in spite of all their prayers. Anne and her mother were just leaving church when they heard the news, but she wanted to go back and pray a bit more for her precious sinner. "I am determined that he shall go to Confession," she insisted. "Let's go and pray some more." And she won the battle.

She was never happy unless she had some special soul to pray for, so when they were at the chateau, she would get the Sisters at Annecy to give her charge of one of their patients whose soul was in danger; and when the winter came and she went down to Cannes, Mother St. Raymond had to provide her with a sinner to take care of. And even now, after her death, bringing hardened sinners back to God seems to be the chief way in which Our Lord is allowing Anne to "spend her Heaven doing good upon earth."

But the apostolate at home lay very close to Anne's heart, closer perhaps than any other. She could not go out and bring sinners back to God, but she could lead her brother and sisters much nearer to His Heart, and this she certainly did.

It is said that a good leader does not tell his men to go forward, he goes himself and only bids them follow. Anne ran on in front of her little band of disciples, there is no doubt about that, but at first she looked round too often to tell them to keep up the pace. Not everybody can keep up with a saint, and budding saints have to learn patience.

Jojo, as we have seen, protested sometimes when Anne reminded him at inconvenient moments that self-denial is a means of attaining perfection. The dinner table is not exactly the place for spiritual admonitions, and she would have been wiser to let him alone in a matter so entirely voluntary, or at least refrain from saying anything in public. She was soon told this, of course, and being a sensible little girl, she quickly learned to be apostolic tactfully and throw all her surplus energy into prayer, but it was a hard trial of patience. How often after this when Jojo would not be good, the poor little mother of his soul would rush off to some corner and pray, for she dared not interfere. Then if he still went on being naughty, she would run up to her own room and climb onto the bed where she could reach the crucifix that hung above. "Jesus," she would beg, "Jesus, dear Jesus, do make Jojo good."

How different was this from the jealousy of her babyhood! The little brother that she had not wanted was now the best loved of all. She would willingly have taken all the blame for his faults upon herself if she had been allowed. Even when he had broken Agnes, one of her favorite dolls, she still tried hard to beg him off.

Jojo had been teasing her by throwing her treasured doll up in the air and catching it again. Anne implored him to stop, for she guessed what would happen before long; but he only laughed and pitched dolly a bit higher to show how well he could catch. The poor child watched with her heart in her mouth till at length the inevitable happened and down came the doll with a crash. Of course Jojo was sorry when the mischief was done, and, also of course, Anne forgave him. But all day she thought about it, fearing that someone would tell their mother when she came in and then Jojo would get a scolding.

A scolding possibly would have done him no harm, but Anne could not bear to think of it, so she made up her mind not to go to sleep till she had explained things to her mother. It was hard work to keep awake, for she was very tired and mother was long in coming, nor did she know her little girl was waiting for her. When at last she came up to the nursery she found a very sleepy Anne rubbing her eyes violently in the effort to keep awake. "Oh, Mother," she cried, "I didn't want to go to sleep till I saw you. Please don't scold Jojo, he didn't do it on purpose." As she said it she fell against her mother's arm, fast asleep, and Madame de Guigné laid the little peacemaker's head gently on the pillow. It had been a brave struggle, for Anne was half dead with sleep, but she would not yield till the cause was gained.

She could not bear to see her little sisters scolded

either. "Perhaps it's my fault, Mother," was the excuse that came so readily to her lips when others were blamed, though nobody was taken in by this, least of all her mother, who knew well enough that whoever was to blame, it was not likely to be Anne.

She was so utterly unselfish over everything that nursery troubles never originated with her. "Anne always forgot herself and never forgot anybody else," Mlle. B. declares. "She seemed to have made up her mind never to lose a chance of being kind." If the others wanted a game, she was as ready to play as if it had been her own choice, and this meant considerable self-denial, for she had strong likes and dislikes which were by no means weakened after she had turned to God. The sensitive little heart felt things as keenly as ever, but now it was the heart of an apostle whose only care was "that God might be honored in all things."[2] What did it matter to her now whether she liked the game or whether the others teased her? "I don't care what they do to me as long as they are good."

There is Anne's spirit, the very same that made St. Paul say: "I will be all things to all men, that I may save all." It was that apostolic love which made dear old St. Philip Neri tell his boys that they might chop wood on his back if they liked, so long as they did not sin. Blessed [now St.] Don Bosco too; he also was an elder brother of little Anne, for he repeated again and again that his boys might wear him out and do what they liked to him,

2. *Rule of St. Benedict,* c. lvii.

"if only they do not offend Our Lord."

And the children knew it. They knew that Anne truly loved God, and just as certainly they knew that she loved them; so though occasionally they had protested a little when she tried to drag them along a bit too fast in the days of her first fervor, yet all three of them trusted her with a confidence that was as much reverence as love. Jojo, in spite of his thoughtlessness, was very much Anne's disciple and turned to her in every difficulty, while the two little sisters would hardly do anything without her.

"When they first came to the convent for catechism," says Mother St. Raymond, "they were very frightened and began to cry. Anne at once guessed what was the matter and asked if she might sit beside them and join their lessons for a time till they had gotten used to things. The little girls cheered up at this and soon began to lose their shyness when they saw that she was quite at home. It was sweet to see how Anne looked after them, foreseeing all their wants and helping them in every way. She stayed with their class for over a month, which must have been very hard for her because it meant not only joining in their lessons when she herself was much further advanced, but also giving up part of her free time which she would certainly rather have spent playing out of doors. It was chiefly owing to her influence that these two became such great friends, because at first they were not inclined to get on very well together, one being quiet and the other lively, but they both agreed in loving

Anne and she drew them together."

But Jojo was her first and best-loved disciple, the one whom she seemed most bent on drawing very close to God. Not only did she go and pray when she saw him tempted, but she would suffer anything to prevent him from losing his temper. One day during the last summer before she died, Jojo ran up to her and said he wanted to play "horse and cart"—with Anne as horse, of course. Poor little sister, she dreaded the game, for she was easily tired and he was tireless. "Oh," she said, "I really *can't* be horse today"—but in the next breath she regained her usual unselfishness and jumped up full of fun, as though she had wanted to play. The game went on literally for hours, too, for the little boy enjoyed driving a willing horse, and Anne ran on cheerfully to the end. And not in vain, for she gained firm hold of her little brother's willful heart, and he would listen to her as to no other, even sometimes when she taught him to deny himself. There was always a strange note of confidence in her voice when she spoke of praying for Jojo. "God must hear me," she used to say, "I am praying that Jojo may be good."

Sometimes in the days when he was still very small, she had even said his prayers for him! This happened occasionally when Madame de Guigné could not accompany them to early Mass. Anne would then edge up to her little brother after Holy Communion and help him make his thanksgiving as she had seen her mother do. A wonderful expression would come over her face as she leaned across to the little boy, whispering in his ear all the beautiful things that filled her own heart. She was so absorbed that she never realized that some cold people close by were warming their own devotion by watching her.

There were other children too, cousins and friends, whom she helped on their way to God. She had such sharp eyes for everybody's troubles. Once some cousins came to stay at the chateau and Anne quickly noticed that one of the older girls looked sad. "I wonder what is the matter with her," she said to Mlle. B. Sympathy, however, did not mean inquisitiveness with her, so she asked no questions. But all through their visit she devoted herself to this particular cousin in the sweetest and most tactful way. "Before we left," writes one of these girls, "little Anne gave us each a present which she had made herself. Some had sketches of the house and garden, others were given small paper knives which she had carved, and one of these was shaped like a cross. 'That is the prettiest,' she said, 'because it is a cross; so I will give it to the eldest of you.' This was the one she had noticed looking sad." That very morning too, she had gotten up early to pick a bunch of flowers for each of them.

Even in the midst of a game she loved, Anne would stop if she thought anyone was getting bored and ask: "Wouldn't you like to play something else? Do tell me what you'd like." If a guest was unhappy, it was not Anne's fault, because charity had made her a perfect hostess before she was six years old. The sweetness of her nature first drew other children to love her, and then gradually they began to understand what it was that made her so kind.

"We went into a chapel once when we were out for a walk," says a little girl who knew Anne. "We were all talking and laughing as we went in, but Anne got serious at once and knelt down. She looked just as if she had found Someone she loved very much and was really talking to Him. When we came out a few minutes later, she began laughing with us just as before."

Most of Anne's friends had seen her pray like that, for when she was out with other children she never failed to persuade them to stop and pray at a wayside shrine or go in to greet Our Lord if they passed a church. And there was always that quick change from light-hearted fun to deep and earnest prayer.

The truth was that Anne's union with God was never interrupted. Her innocent fun went up as incense for His glory no less than her work, for the fire of charity consumed every action, even the most trivial.

It was for Him she played, not merely to amuse herself. Indeed, her own share of the fun was often self-denial and sometimes even physical suffering, as we have already seen. But this tiredness, which she bore so willingly to please others, taught her to be tenderly thoughtful when she was out with those who were weaker than herself. "Jojo, don't go so fast, the little ones can't keep up with us," she often whispered to her brother when they had the two little sisters with them, for she could not bear to see them tired or suffering in any way.

Very often in the winter when she felt cold during the night, Anne would get up, not to put something extra on her own bed, but to take the
eiderdown and cover her sisters with it. Is it any
wonder that they loved her and were willing to let
her lead them to God?

It was the same at the catechism class; all the
other children loved Anne, so much in fact, that
they all wanted to sit beside her! She, in her innocence, could not think why.

"Mother," she said, "why do all the little girls in
the class want to sit by me?"

"Because they are kind, dearie, and want to be
nice to you," answered Madame de Guigné, who
did not wish her to be flattered by it. She need
not have feared; Anne was already too humble to
guess that the others spoke of her as "the nicest of
all." She only thought they were very kind and
tried more than ever to repay it.

The de Guigné children only went to the convent for the catechism class, so Anne had not so
much opportunity of influencing her companions
there as she could at home; but even the short
time she spent with them was enough to make these
little ones realize that there was something very
special about her. They loved her because she was
so sweet, but they reverenced her too.

"Look out, Nenette is coming, we must not shock
her." This was a warning that often went round
during the free time. The children knew Anne was
holy. It was not long before the sharpest of them

began to see how it was that this little newcomer got on so much better than they did. Her natural quickness counted for something, of course,[3] but the remarkable thing about Anne was that she really *worked*, even as a tiny child of five.

Catechism to her was not merely a lesson, but a chance of finding out something more about what her dear Jesus had taught, and therefore it was an absorbing interest to her. But Mlle. B. says she was just as willing to work over studies that she did not care for at all, and even those she found very unpleasant. Multiplication and spelling, for instance, were anything but joy to poor little Anne, who suffered from frequent headaches; but she attacked her difficulties bravely and from a purely supernatural motive. And what was this motive? She expressed it once to a friend: "Our work is a present that we can give Jesus. So when it seems hard, just think that now you have something for Him. Nothing costs much when we love Him."

Almost in the same words she wrote down her own resolution after a retreat: "I will imitate the little Jesus." (It is worth noting that Anne did not say: "I ought," or "I wish," to imitate Him, but "I *will*." That iron will which had once made her mother fear for the child's future was now a powerful instrument in God's hands, by which the little one "fulfilled a long life in a short space.") "If the time (in class) seems long, I will offer God the *effort*."

Again she wrote: "God will say to me: 'I want

_____

3. She had learned to read in a month.

you to be more obedient, I do not want you more
vain. If you are so at your age, what will you be
later on?" . . . A child who disobeys her parents
and her teachers, who is willful, jealous and lazy,
will serve God badly. She will not do His Will.

"My soul is meant for Heaven. We take a lot of
trouble over dressing our bodies but think much
less about our souls. . . . There ought to be: First,
cleanness (of soul), which means avoiding sin. Second, proper clothing, that is, doing our duty. Third,
adornment, which means the good actions that we
do of our own free will. . . . It depends on me,
Mother cannot do the work for me."

All this was written in 1921 when Anne was ten
years old; but it was not by any means a new program, for she had written much the same after other
retreats, always with the same clear, practical sense.
With humility, too, for when she was nine she wrote
these resolutions for imitating Our Lord: "How shall
I do it? How shall I overcome the obstacles? . . .
These are my faults: I am inclined to be proud and
to be lazy, so a *daily* struggle is necessary for me."[4]

There was nothing sentimental about Anne. Her
ideas about following Our Lord were just as plain
and straight as His own simple command: "If you
love Me, keep My Commandments." She did love

---

4. These resolutions were entirely Anne's own choice. Mother
St. Raymond used to make a few suggestions to some of
the smaller children during their retreats, but she saw that
Anne fully understood what was said, and therefore very
wisely let her alone; so these notes are Anne's own thoughts
expressed in her own words.

Him and so she meant to do what He asked of her.

It sounds like a very simple program, but so few people have the strength to be really simple. They go a long way around by following an elaborate plan of their own and invent artificial hardships which have no place in Our Lord's plan at all. Instead of concentrating on the things He cared about most, and offering Him the perfect fulfillment of the precept of charity, they want to do something "different from the rest of men," and then they have neither time nor energy to be kind. Anne had time to be kind. Like her Lord, she "had compassion on the multitude," and so she spent herself for others as He had done. Her "multitude" was smaller certainly, for she seldom had a chance to help anyone outside her own little circle; but what she could do, she did, for the love of her Lord and God.

When very young, Anne had given Him her heart with all the love of which she was capable. But during the last summer of her life she began to be conscious of a definite desire to be a nun. For years, one of her favorite prayers had been: "Little Jesus, my sweet Saviour, keep my heart all for Yourself," and now her thoughts began to turn towards the religious life as a practical possibility.

Like so many other children who love the Little Flower, she was first attracted to the Carmelites. But whatever order she might have joined in later years, it is very evident that even then, though she was still too young to understand the full significance of a nun's life, she realized that it meant the complete gift of herself to God.

"One would have said she had already made the three vows," wrote Mother St. Raymond, "even Poverty, for she lived truly poor in the midst of wealth." It was most remarkable how Anne managed to get the worst of everything for herself; she was so skillful in "arranging" for the others to have the best and prettiest when there was any question of choice. Only a deliberate intention of living poorly, as far as was possible, could explain her systematic effort to keep everything that was for her own use as simple as her mother would allow.

Strange to say, she understood economy too, which is somewhat remarkable in a child brought up in such easy circumstances. But the fact is undeniable, for all witnesses agree that she was most careful of everything she used and, what is still more unusual (even among grownups!), she was exceedingly careful of other people's things. Perhaps it was that the thought of her precious "poor" was never very far from Anne's mind. For their sake she had learned to value even trifles, so she would eagerly seize upon any pieces of fabric that were left over when anything was being made, and out of these bits she often manufactured wonderful little gifts for the poor people she loved so much.

Purity she loved intensely and practiced perfectly in every way that a child of ten could understand it. "The joy of a pure conscience was hers," writes one witness; "it shone from her." "She had a certain reserve," says another, "which did not in any way prevent her from being so affectionate that

everyone loved her." In spite of her liveliness and
love of fun, Anne always kept full control over herself, even in the midst of the wildest games. Kindly
thoughtful for others, she did not lose sight of obedience either. "Oh no!" she panted when nearly
caught during an exciting game of hide and seek,
"we mustn't hide there. Grandpa said we would ruin
the flowers."

"I have never seen her act on impulse," Mother
St. Raymond says. There was always that self-pos-
session in her which revealed the command she
had won over her natural instincts.

"Who is that child?" asked a nun who had met
Anne for the first time. "Her expression is wonderful. One can see Jesus in her eyes. It was unfor-
gettable, the strange mixture of innocence and
gravity in those clear eyes."[5]

And then there was obedience. What can one
say of that? Was not Anne's whole life a continual "Yes" to all that her Lord asked of her?

After that first retreat when she heard that "Obedience is the sanctity of children," she made the
resolution to obey perfectly as the Child Jesus had
done, and all those who have lived with Anne tell
us that she kept her word.

Even as a tiny child she seemed to realize that
obedience is a treasure house of grace, which it is
sad to lose. Possibly she had heard something of
that sort in a sermon, but Anne must have thought

---

5. Her eyes were brown, but very clear, so her mother says.
Her hair was fair at first, but grew darker.

it over in her own mind, for she occasionally came out with one of those surprisingly direct remarks that can only originate in the simplicity of a child's logic.

Not long after her First Communion, Anne happened to hear that priests working on the foreign missions were obliged to have beards. She thought about this for a little while, apparently puzzling over some problem, then she looked up and said: "But supposing their beards won't grow. What do they do then? Do they have to lose a chance of obeying?"

Obviously Anne thought obedience was something rather precious. And so, because she always wished to share her precious things, she became the Apostle of the nursery in this also; for not content with obeying perfectly herself, she often tried to smooth the way of obedience for the other children when she saw they were going to find it difficult.

Once the children were invited to a wedding, and among the many good things to eat there were sherbets; but Madame de Guigné, for some good reason doubtless, told them that they were not to take any. Immediately there were three very long faces, but Anne accepted the little sacrifice with a smile and soon persuaded the others to obey more cheerfully, even if they could not manage to laugh over it as she did.

Staying in bed for a cold was another trial which Anne contrived to make more pleasant—and more sanctifying, perhaps! She and Marinette were the victims who were condemned to bed for having colds—and on a Sunday, too! But Anne's cheerfulness was undaunted. She got her missal, and the two little girls sang right through the Mass with as much voice as they could produce.

It is worth remarking, perhaps, that Anne had a great appreciation for her missal. She prayed to Our Lord in her own way, of course, but she loved to think over the beautiful things she saw in her book, as the following story shows.

It was a hot dusty day in summer, Madame de Guigné says, and Jojo was very unwilling to go to Vespers. Anne heard him giving vent to his feelings as they made their way along the road, so after a bit she looked at her missal to see what she could find. (French missals frequently have Vespers in them.) She happened to open it at Psalm 42 (*Judica*), but the place did not matter much, for she only wanted to show Jojo how beautiful the prayers were when you really stopped to think what they meant.

"Look," she said, "if you read your book, you will see how lovely the prayers are. Listen to this: 'I will go to the altar of God, God who will fill my soul with a joy ever new.' Do you understand that? Isn't it beautiful? God who fills my soul with a joy always new"! And so she went on explaining the Psalm in her own words, a proof that she, at least, understood how to use the prayers of the Church.

But to go back to the subject of obedience. It happened once during the hunting season that their mother thought it better that only Jojo should go to the meet and not the little girls. This time the disappointment was almost too much even for Anne, and she ran away and hid herself, for she could not help crying a little. In a few minutes, however, she had recovered her equilibrium and came back to Mademoiselle smiling bravely.

"I expect Mother is right," she said; "she must have had some reason for not letting us go too. Anyhow, I'm glad Jojo has gone." Then turning around she saw that the two little sisters were also in tears. That was enough. Anne was herself again in a moment.

"Oh, don't cry," she whispered, "we're going to have a lovely time while he's away. Come along and play a game." The nursery soon brightened up now that Anne was her own cheerful self once more, and everybody forgot there was such a thing in the world as a hunt; but who can doubt that the Angels recorded that morning's sacrifice by adding a big figure to Anne's credit in the Book of Life.

The Angels! How she loved her own Angel. Only in the next world shall we know how much he did for Anne. "Ask your Angel to help you," she often said to her sisters when she saw there was likely to be trouble; and who can doubt that she practiced what she preached?

Her influence over these two little ones was very great, so it is hardly surprising that before long one of them began to think that she too would like to be a nun when she grew up. Anne, of course, was delighted when she heard this and started to explain all her own plans. "We must practice the sort of things we shall have to do when we enter the convent," she said; and the disciple was only too ready to imitate everything her leader did.

As far as spirituals were concerned, they were not far wrong; but occasionally the two little aspirants to religious life did some curious things by way of "practicing." Once they were found in the dairy solemnly inhaling deep breaths over a new cheese. When asked what they were doing, Anne explained that they were smelling the cheese "because it isn't very nice." This was intended to be mortification!

During the last year of her life Anne had the great joy of discovering another future nun among her friends. This little girl was about her own age and she could talk to her about all these things in a way that her sister was too much of a baby to understand, for Anne had very clear and definite ideas as to what it meant to be consecrated to God. Her childish years might occasionally prompt her to invent a funny form of mortification, but when it came to speaking of the inner spirit of religious life, many an old nun might have felt that Anne was as far above her as this little friend did.

"Nenette had such love of God that I simply can't describe it," she said after Anne's death, when she was asked to give testimony of her friend's sanctity. Almost in tears, the little girl told how during those last few months of her life, Anne had seemed to realize that her time was short, for she

spoke continually of Heaven as if it was the one
thing she longed for. Only the remembrance of her
vocation made her hesitate, because she knew
something of the great merit of a long life spent
in the service of God. The year before, when she
was only nine, she had said to Mademoiselle: "A
long life is a blessing, because there would be time
to suffer a great deal for Our Lord," but now all
that was past. Earthly hopes, even the holiest, were
slipping away, and the child looked beyond her
vocation towards that final End to which all voca-
tions lead.

Anne's desire of consecrating herself to Our Lord
was singularly pure from any trace of self-seeking.
When asked why she wished to be a nun, she would
answer with a simple gravity that was most impres-
sive: "I want to be a nun for the glory of God."[6]

This being so, it is easy to understand why she
was so anxious to share her vocation with others.
The more souls she could persuade to love Him
alone, the more glory she could give to her beloved
Lord. That was Anne's view, and so she spoke more
and more eagerly as her time grew short, for she

---

6. This sentence, so magnificent in its simplicity, goes down
   to the essentials of sanctity, and it was no chance remark.
   Anne's love of God was so selfless that it necessarily showed
   itself in zeal for His glory. How often she used to say: "God
   surely must hear this prayer because it is for His glory."
   This was why she insisted that her sinners must be converted and wanted to go on praying till they were!
     Even as a tiny child she had instinctively loved the prayer
   Gloria Patri, because it was all for God, and she used to
   say it on every bead of her Rosary sometimes.

wanted to feel sure that this special friend would take her place in a convent and serve Our Lord as she herself had meant to do. The little girl was often surprised at her friend's insistence, because Anne was not at all ill and there seemed no reason why she should be so anxious to make sure of a future that was still so distant for both of them. But it was no use arguing with Anne; she went on persisting that M. . . must promise to take her place in a convent if she herself should die; so at length, awed by such earnestness, the child gave her word.

Chapter 5

THE END OF THE CLIMB

WHEN a soul that truly seeks God is drawing near to her journey's end, a certain calm serenity comes over her, very much like the stillness of an evening at the end of summer, when the great heats are over and the grain stands ripe for cutting.

So it was with Anne. During those summer days of 1921 and on through the autumn, all who knew her best wondered more and more at the strangely sweet peace which seemed to be filling her soul. The full splendor of God's work is hidden from the eyes of men, but some small fringes of the glory can be seen—and that little is very wonderful.

Did Anne know she was so near her journey's end? Though there is no reason for thinking that she had any exact knowledge of the date of her death, it is certain that some instinctive feeling must have warned her that it was near, for she persisted so earnestly that M. . . must promise to take her place as a nun "if I should die." This little friend had no doubt about it at all. "I shall never see her again," she said sadly after she left Anne that autumn. "I am sure God is going to take her; she doesn't seem to belong to this world any more."

She had felt awed and deeply impressed by the way Anne talked of Heaven as though it were a place she was going to see very soon and could hardly wait for the day to come when she would be there.

All those who knew Anne well are convinced that she must have had some knowledge of what was to come. Mother St. Raymond thinks that during those months she was making her last sacrifice, the most costly of all, which God asked as the crown of her life. She realized that to die she must leave her mother.

That autumn Anne was so unusually tender to Madame de Guigné. It seemed as if she were trying to give her a big store of love to fall back on when the great grief came. She knew well that to go to God she must leave that dear little mother whom she loved so intensely, and grieve her terribly in her passing, but she said nothing. Possibly she remembered a certain conversation one day long ago when she was only seven. Madame de Guigné tells the story:

"I had asked Anne what she said to Our Lord when she prayed, and she answered simply: 'I tell Him that I love Him, and then I talk about you and I ask Him to make the others good. I ask Him lots of things and I pray for my sinners too.' Then she stopped, her face reddened and she looked up at me a little doubtfully as if wondering how I would take what she was going to say, but she went on: 'And I tell Him that I want to see Him.' A stab of fear went through my heart, and I could not help crying out: 'Oh, my darling, but what do

you think I shall feel like if you go to see Our
Lord?'

"But my little one knew what she had said. 'Oh
yes, Mother, I have thought about it,' she answered,
'and I don't want to make you sad, but Daddy is
in Heaven and you will soon go there too and so
will the others. We are all meant to go there.'"

But though she spoke so firmly, Anne evidently
realized that she had pointed a sword at her
mother's heart that day and she would not do it
again. Even during the last days of her illness when
she knew that death was very near, she never spoke
of it when her mother was in the room. She only
became, if possible, more tenderly thoughtful.

Ever since that morning in 1915 when sorrow
had shown Anne that life is nothing but the way
to God, she had wanted her mother to think of
that only home where there are no partings. How
often she lifted her mother's eyes to Heaven when
she saw them full of tears, and always with the
Angel's message of triumph: "Why seek ye the living among the dead?"

"Daddy is happy," the baby of four would whisper when she saw her mother brooding over her
grief; "he is happy, Mother darling; he is in Heaven
and we shall go to him."

"Anne fully realized what any allusion to the war
meant to me," writes Madame de Guigné. "If we
saw an officer home from the front or anyone spoke
of the war, she would come up to me and whisper
in my ear: 'Remember, he is happy; he is in
Heaven.' Her loving little heart was always on the

watch. Even in the midst of a game, she would stop if she heard a word about the war and run up to me with her word of comfort."

Anne always looked upwards in trouble, any trouble, big or small. Her mother bears witness to it. "How often she used to say when she saw any-one worried: 'Why fret about things? God is there. If He allows it, surely it must be good for us.'"

In 1917, when so many of the prisoners in Germany were exchanged, desperate hopes rose in the hearts of the war widows, and not unreasonably, for some of the "dead" turned out to be simply "missing," and some of the "widows" could cast off their veils. Is it any wonder that even Madame de Guigné dared to hope again in spite of the apparent certainty of her husband's death? So many mistakes had been made about others, might there not be at least a possibility of his return? She said nothing, of course, to the children, but Anne quickly guessed her mother's thoughts and was ready this time with more than a word of comfort. She was ill at the moment with a sharp attack of some sort of rheumatic pain, very hard for a child of six to bear, but Anne's spirit was that of St. Louis, and she said: "Mother, if somebody must suffer to get Daddy back, I'm so glad it's me." She was ready to offer sharp pain to God as her father's ransom.

But this wild hope passed, and then Armistice Day came to send the world mad with joy. The news came late to the old chateau hidden among the hills of Savoy, but as the sun was setting that November afternoon, the bells of Annecy-le-Vieux

pealed out the message of peace that had been so
long in coming.

Madame de Guigné was in the park with her
family when the peal of victory broke the stillness
of the woods. She knew what it meant. The years
of struggle were over at last and peace was ringing
through the land. Peace to all men and joy to most,
but a fresh sword in the heart of a war widow. The
bells of many nations were ringing round the world
for a victory won by death.

That was what Armistice Day meant to the little family at the chateau, and not only to them.
In every land that day there were tears amid the
cheering. But Anne looked up through her tears
to the land where all are victors. "Daddy is in
Heaven, Mother darling," she whispered softly,
"don't cry; remember how happy he is, he is happy
forever, and he will never be sad again." She would
have liked to stay with her mother, but it was getting late and the children had to go in. Anne
obeyed as usual, but that night she would not sleep.
Sitting up stiffly, she waited wide awake to give
one last word of comfort when Madame de Guigné
came for their good-night kiss. "Oh, Mother darling, don't you be sad anymore," begged the little
one. "Daddy is so happy, he can see us, he loves
us and you know we shall go to him someday."

During this trying time the children were told
to be careful to spare their mother as much as possible and above all not to worry her in any way.
It would have been better not to have told Anne
anything of that sort, for she was only too much

inclined to wear herself out for her mother's sake
and hide any pain she might have, for fear of wor-
rying her.

It was just about this time that she slipped on
the ice and strained one of the muscles of her knee.
Madame de Guigné ran to pick her up, for she saw
that Anne was trying in vain to rise. The child
was seriously hurt and she had gone white with
pain, but though tears were in her eyes, not a cry
came from her lips, nor so much as an exclama-
tion. It was not her own hurt that worried Anne.
"I'm so sorry to have frightened you," were her first
words. "I'm all right. It's nothing." She was only
seven, and a fall means much to a little girl.

Anne was no stranger to pain, for though a
healthy enough child on the whole, she had had
two serious illnesses during her early years, and
when she was about eight, severe headaches caused
by spinal weakness came to try her patience and
make school work a difficulty. She did not complain if her head got bad in class, nor did she sit
still and do nothing. She used to go on trying to
work until Mother St. Raymond noticed that she
did not look well and asked if she had a headache.
Then the child would say simply: "Yes, Mother,"
and go at once when she was told to lie down. The
lying down must have been almost as much of a
trial as the headache it was supposed to cure, for
the doctor had ordered her to lie flat on a board
when the pain came on, and Anne obeyed perfectly, as usual. "I often wondered at her patience,"
says Mother St. Raymond. "Very few children would

have lain still like that on a board without a word of complaint and for such a long time . . . but Anne never stopped to think whether a thing was pleasant or not if she knew it was the will of God, either for some reason of duty or necessity, or for the good of others. Her will ruled all her actions so that there was perfect order in her life. It was very striking to see such a brave will in such a frail little body."

Perhaps it might be as well to give here a few words from Mother St. Raymond's summing up of Anne's character:

"She understood so well that there is no other reason for our life on earth except to go to God. To go to God all the time—that was her life. She went to Him in all her actions. . . I have known many good children, but never one so perfect in every way as Anne was. In each of them there was some weak point, but in her I could see none. . . The more I think of her virtues, the more I realize that she must have completely renounced herself.

"Some people have said to me: 'Oh, that child was pushed into sanctity, overdirected, etc.' This is not true. Anne had nothing more than the rest. I gave her practically no special advice . . . but most children do not take much notice of general admonitions, while she obeyed at once and completely. That was the remarkable thing about her.

"When she first came to us, Mother St. Joseph[1]

---

1. Madame de Guigné's sister and M. St. Raymond's superior.

was asked to help the child a little and teach her to pray, but Anne's aunt was too wise. 'What good should I do?' she said to me. 'I should only spoil her simplicity. God teaches that child.'

"Those who think children can be forced or persuaded into sanctity show that they have had very little experience with children. One cannot force a child's soul. To attempt to do so would probably make the poor little thing take a dislike to religion altogether. Certainly Anne was not forced. The truth is this. God gave her grace and she corresponded to it with the whole of her will."

Surely here Mother St. Raymond has given us "the truth, the whole truth, and nothing but the truth."

Many children have had great graces, but how many use their grace as Anne did? The child's fidelity in the trials of daily life was so nearly complete that the only word which seems to describe it adequately is that which the Church alone can use officially, namely, heroism.

It is that asceticism in little things which makes such a very great thing.

Though the spinal trouble was supposed to have been cured, Anne's headaches came back with renewed force about the beginning of December, 1921; but at first there seemed no cause for anxiety, as the doctor did not think very seriously of them. Anne was a little quieter than usual, that was all; and as she could not play, she used to sit out in the garden beside Mademoiselle. It was very lovely there under the trees looking out over the blue Mediterranean, and the little maid seemed radiantly happy in spite of her pain.

Perhaps she was happy because she had made her sacrifice, for one day after speaking of her mother, she said: "We have lots of joys here on earth, but they do not last; the only joy that lasts is to have made a sacrifice." Mademoiselle had some experience of spiritual things, and as she listened to the child, the conviction deepened in her mind that Anne was very close to God. That indescribable expression which so many had seen in her eyes came more often now and it was more wonderful.

On All Saints Day, a lady saw her kneeling in church "transfigured," as she described it. She was at some distance, but she left her place in order to look more closely at the little face that was, as she said, "more than human." Another day, someone who did not know Anne at all happened to look up just as the child came out of the confessional and she was so struck by her expression that she asked the priest who that little girl was.

"Why do you want to know?" asked Anne's confessor.

"Why, Father," replied the lady, "because she looked positively transfigured when she came out."

"Transfigured" was certainly the word; there was something so heavenly about her. That radiant look could come from no earthly happiness, and those who loved her feared, for they felt that such a soul would not pass easily to her glory. Nor were they wrong.

But the days went by and Anne was no worse. Everyone supposed that if she kept quiet, these headaches would pass off as they had done before, and so no great anxiety was felt, though at times she suffered severely. This was especially the case when she had to go in a motor car. Possibly it was the vibration, for 1921 cars were not so smooth running as those of the present day; but whatever the cause may have been, motoring meant for Anne an increase of pain in her head and acute pain in her back.

But sometimes these journeys by car were unavoidable and Anne knew this, so she made the best of it in her usual way by trying to help others. The motion of the car also made one of her little sisters feel sick just then, and she used to take Marinette on her lap, so that the little one might be more comfortable. It was noticed sometimes that she held her rosary in the other hand when she was holding Marinette, praying perhaps to "Our Lady of Consolation." Very often during these last weeks they heard Anne singing the *Ave Maris Stella* as she went about the house.

On the 19th a change came. The children had been out that afternoon at La Nartassiere,[2] visiting Mlle. B.'s family, who noticed that Anne was quieter than usual but did not suspect that there was anything wrong. When she came down to dinner that evening, however, the pain in her head suddenly became so severe that the poor child had

___

2. The home of Mademoiselle's parents.

to go upstairs again without eating anything.

"Poor Nenette, is it very bad?" asked one of her sisters as she left the room.

"Yes," she answered quietly, *"but it will soon be over."*

"Soon," perhaps, as God sees things, but it was to be longer and more terrible than many a martyrdom.

At first the doctor did not think too seriously of the case, provided she was kept very quiet in bed; so for the first few days there was no great anxiety in the house and Christmastide passed fairly happily. For Anne the Holy Night brought a first glimpse of Heaven. After her Confession on Christmas Eve, Anne's face was lit up again with that supernatural expression which made her look, as people said, "transfigured." It was her last moment on Thabor before she reached Calvary.

Only three days later, on December 27, the hopes of those who loved her were dashed to the ground. That morning when the doctor arrived, her mother thought Anne was still sleeping, but he quickly saw that the little one was in a state of coma. It was meningitis, and he did not hide his anxiety.

But by midday she was conscious again and the pain in her head and back became intolerable. Her face went livid and was so contorted by agony that it was heart-rending to look at her. She knew it well enough, poor child; and unselfish to the last, she thought first of others, for she realized how it hurt them to see her in such a state. She would thank them so sweetly each time the cold compress on her head was renewed, and this was continual during the bad attacks of pain. In fact, her mother says that all through her illness Anne was always thanking them for every little thing done for her, so often indeed, that it became necessary to tell her she must *not* say "Thank you" so many times.

Next day, the feast of the Holy Innocents, her confessor came again to hear Anne's Confession. When she had finished he asked if she would like to receive Holy Communion.

"Oh, *yes*," sighed the child.

"Never shall I forget that word," the priest wrote long after. "The whole desire of her soul was in it."

As he went out of the room Anne called him back, for she remembered that she had not thanked him. To the last she would be courteous.

Then she lay with eyes closed, waiting for the coming of Our Lord. So still was she that Father G. . . was startled when he returned with the Blessed Sacrament. Had death come faster than he had? Bending over the bed, he said distinctly:

"Here is Our Lord, my little one. Do you want to receive Him?"

Then the child's eyes opened. Once again came that whispered "Yes," intense with all the love of her life.

A little later Extreme Unction was proposed, but Anne only smiled up at the priest with something of her old brightness. "I understand, Father," she said, "but I know I am not ill enough for that yet."

She was indeed quite ill enough, but the priest did
not insist. "She seemed so certain about it and so
sure of herself," writes Father G. . . "that I shared
her confidence."

Two days later, however, Madame de Guigné
thought it wiser to have her anointed, and the
parish priest came to give Extreme Unction.

Anne had no fear of the Last Sacraments. Long
ago, when quite a little girl, she had been astonished to hear that some people are afraid to men-
tion Extreme Unction to a dying person for fear of
frightening him. "Surely that can't be true?" she
said. "Why, I would *want* to receive the Last Sacraments if I was dying. I wouldn't be afraid!" And
she was not. Tortured with almost unendurable pain
as she was on that 30th of December, Anne had
the energy not only to follow the details of the
ceremony, but to ask questions about it too. "They
use the oil of the sick for Extreme Unction, don't
they?" she asked. "I don't think it is the same as
the oil of catechumens, is it?"

Very early she had understood that it was the
Holy Spirit Himself who taught the Apostles how
to give the Sacraments, and so she always loved to
see them administered, for with that unerring
instinct of the pure of heart, Anne realized how
well the outward sign expresses the inward grace.

It is rather curious that Extreme Unction was
the only Sacrament not mentioned during that
famous examination by the Superior of the Jesuits.
Perhaps he shrank from speaking of the last anoint-
ing to such a little child. But the years had passed—

so few of them—and now that Sacrament which comes but once to most of us had come for Anne. Unafraid, the child lay still, quietly attentive as the priest sealed the members of her body before it should be laid aside until that day when "all things bloom afresh."[3]

But New Year's Day came, and Anne was no worse. In fact she brightened up a little and the family began to breathe again. Perhaps God was hearing their prayers and meant to give them the life of their little girl as the most welcome of New Year gifts. Madame de Guigné even had a Mass of thanksgiving said, for human hearts are very elastic, and Anne was so bright that it seemed just possible she might throw it off after all. She roused all her energy that day, wishing everyone a happy New Year and doing her best to make them forget her illness. She even asked to see all the maids, and in spite of the pain caused by the slightest movement, she forced herself to lean forward and kiss each one.

But this was the last flash. Only a day or two later the doctor found that without any congestion of the lungs, her chest muscles were paralyzed, and for some days the poor child had attacks of suffocation which lasted hours at a time. Bravely she fought for breath without a sign of impatience. Years ago when she was in great pain someone had said

---

3. "*Dies venit, dies tua,*
   In qua reflorent omnia."
   —Lauds hymn in Lent.

pityingly: "Poor little Nenette, you do suffer bravely." And the child had answered: "Oh no, I'm only learning to suffer."

The lesson had been well learned by this time. Never did she complain; and only occasionally, when utterly exhausted, was she heard to sigh very softly: "Oh, dear Lord, I'm *absolutely* done!" The fastest runner must stop sometimes to take breath. It was only that, as those around her knew too well, but Anne would be penitent, fearing she had failed in patience. It was her one fear. Never, of her own accord, did she pray to be cured, for she knew God wanted her, but often she would ask the nurse if she had been patient enough, if she had borne the pain well. One day when she was half delirious they heard her cry for forgiveness, for strength.

"Have I been faithful, Lord? Little Jesus, I'm afraid I haven't been brave. I've not prayed enough." Then would come the prayers for Confession and the Act of Contrition. Once they heard her murmur: "Dear St. Anne, have pity on my sins."

But most of the time she was perfectly lucid, offering her pain in full consciousness "for the glory of God," as she had desired to offer her life in religion. And each day she renewed the offering, sometimes each hour, especially for the conversion of her "dear sinners."

Once after a terrible crisis, Madame de Guigné bent over the child's bed and whispered to her: "You *have* been brave, darling. This will comfort the Heart of Our Lord and win over some of your sinners." The torture had wrung no word from Anne, but now she gasped for joy.

"Oh, Mother, I'm so glad. If it does that, I will bear lots more."

Though Anne did not think she would be cured and did not want to be, she never grieved her mother by refusing to join in the prayers that were said for her recovery, but she always added: "Please cure other sick people too." She was specially interested in three small children whom her doctor was attending just then. Each day when he came Anne would ask how they were getting on and whether they would soon be better. It cut him to the heart to hear this sweet child ask that, for he knew better than anyone what she was suffering with such amazing courage. He knew too that there would be no getting better for Anne. She had gone beyond the skill of doctors now. And so one day when she asked how the children were getting on, he answered sharply:

"They're not so good as you are; that's what's the matter with them!"

But Anne's heart was so near Heaven now that earthly praises sounded very far away, so far off as to seem unreal. She was not flattered; she simply said: "I expect they are more ill than I am, or perhaps they haven't got such a kind mother."

At last came the news that these children were very much better. It was just at the time when she herself was going deeper and deeper into very terrible suffering, but she appeared to be delighted. There was never a moan over her own condition, nor a prayer for relief.

Still she thought of everyone and everything, dreading lest people were getting tired through nursing her. From the moment Anne's illness became serious Madame de Guigné rarely left her precious little girl either night or day, but others were there too. Mademoiselle and a great friend of the family helped her in the nursing, and Anne was very worried about them all. She did not at all like anyone to sit up at night with her, probably not realizing that it was absolutely necessary. Once she woke up and saw Mademoiselle still beside the bed.

"Oh," she exclaimed, "why are you still there? Do go to bed. You will be so tired. I am sure Mother would be cross if she knew."

A few days later they got a trained nurse, one of the Bon Secours nuns who assist the sick in their homes, and Anne was just as anxious about her when she found that the Sister meant to sit up all night. She used to be quite distressed if she woke and saw her by the bed.

"Why, Sister dear," she would say, "I really don't want you to stay beside me, you will get so tired."

Then as another thought struck her:

"You must be hungry, too."

Once she added the helpful remark:

"Won't you take a bit of that sugar?" Anne was still a very little girl!

Towards the end there was not much waking, for she hardly slept at all. They used to tell her to try to sleep, of course, and she would do her best, poor child, by shutting her eyes; but sleep was less obedient than Anne.

Another thing which worried her very much was that those who watched by her could not have their meals at the proper time. She understood after a while that it was no use protesting, but she found it difficult to realize that people were only too glad to stay and take care of her.

The fact was, Anne was too humble to have any idea of how much she was loved. When Madame de Guigné told her that the Sisters at Annecy were praying very hard for her, she said: "I suppose it's because they're so fond of you and they know you're worried about me."

"Oh no, darling," her mother answered quickly, "the Sisters love you because you have been a good little girl with them."

Anne sighed. "If I've been good there, it's only because you taught me."

She was quite sincere when she said things like that. No one who had come in contact with Anne would ever suspect her of saying anything for effect, even in a weak moment, for her whole character was absolutely straightforward and she knew no fear.

She was genuinely surprised when some of the children she had known at the convent came to ask about her. "They are kind," she said. "I wonder what made them think of me." But how could people help thinking of her, when she thought of everybody?

One would expect her to remember Marinette's seventh birthday on January 4, which of course she did and made as much of it as was possible for her to do. But she also remembered when it was time for the two little girls to start going to the catechism class again after the holidays. They would have to go without their little mother now, and Anne had some misgivings. "Don't let them go alone yet," she said to her mother. "I'm so afraid they will get into mischief."

And so she went on from day to day, but all things have an end, and the vital forces of that poor little body were nearly exhausted. Those four weeks were in very truth the holocaust of all that had been Anne. She was, as she said, "absolutely done."

Two days before her death, one of the nuns came to see Anne. Mademoiselle was sitting by the bed at the time, but she went out of the room when the visitor entered. A few minutes later, the nun came out again in tears, saying: "I do thank God for having allowed me to see that child. She is indeed a Saint. Her face looks simply angelic." Mademoiselle was rather surprised, because when she had left Anne a few minutes before, the poor child's face had been contorted with pain and so drawn out of its proper shape that it was painful to look at her. This contraction was quite involuntary, and, as we have already seen, Anne herself realized that it was not pleasant to look at her when the muscles were drawn up like that. "I went quickly back to the room," says Mlle. B., "and found Anne completely changed. Her face was indeed lovely. She lay there sweetly smiling." It was near the end. Anne had passed through the storm, and as she turned into port, the lights of the City of God shone across the quiet waters and lit up her face.

She lay smiling; but suddenly she cried out excitedly: "Jojo, Leleine, Baby, come and see. Oh, look how beautiful it is!" What was it she saw? God knows.

But the next day she was more explicit. "I was standing by her bed," says Madame de Guigné, "when she suddenly told me her Guardian Angel was there. 'There, Mother, there behind you. Turn around and you will see him.' She said this twice over. In the course of the day we thought more than once that we would lose her, and the prayers for the dying were said. Anne was perfectly conscious and answered the invocations. I am quite sure she knew she was dying, but she still said nothing to me, for she could not bear to hurt me. Only once, when she was in great pain and I said the doctor would soon come and do something to ease her, she looked at me and said gently: 'He can do nothing more for me.'"

During that night, when her life in this world was almost burned out, Anne's soft little voice was heard again. She was saying the Act of Hope. Twice over she said it, there in the face of death. She knew in Whom she had believed, and she was certain. . . . It was the supreme act of homage, perfect trust at the moment when all tangible things are slipping—the moment between Heaven and earth, when trust is of all else the most precious in the sight of God. And Anne gave it, gave it completely, as she had given all things. She was ready now. Her day was at hand, the 14th of January, her "birthday in Heaven."

She turned to the nurse and said: "Sister, may I go to the Angels?"

Then, as the nun bade her go, she sighed softly: "Oh, thank you, thank you."

She said no more to those on earth, but once again she spoke—to her Mother in Heaven. She could not look up to Mary's picture, for her eyes were partly paralyzed, but word for word the child repeated Our Lady's anthem, *Hail Holy Queen*.

Anne's time was now at hand. But as her eyes were closing on this life, the Doctor was touched by the sight of Madame de Guigné's grief, and bending over the child, he said: "Look once more at your mother, dear."

And Anne, obedient even in death, lifted her eyelids with a last effort and looked at her mother with a look that is burned into her soul forever. Then she sank into that sleep from which the Angels were to wake her.

Chapter 6

AT THE TOP

THE climb was over. Anne had reached the top and gone to meet God.

On earth, there was peace around that bedside, and a joy even in the mother's heart, that was to grow sweeter with the passing years. "I felt her near us, so living and so happy," writes one who loved Anne exceedingly, "that somehow I could not be sad."

Yet the poor little body lay there, very still and pale, clothed in the white robe of the dead, simple and unadorned, for no flowers even were allowed to soften the majesty of death. But the hearts of those that loved her were not deceived. That worn-out form was no longer Anne. She had no need of flowers; she was living, vitally living, living surely as she had never lived before. *"Tuis enim fidelibus, Domine, vita mutatur, non tollitur."*[1]

*   *   *

All through those days, friends of the family passed and repassed in that quiet room, and from each one came the same words: "She is a Saint.

---

1. "For Thy faithful ones, O Lord, life is not taken away, but changed."—*Preface from the Mass of the Dead.*

We should pray *to* her, not *for* her." But of out-
siders there were not many, for Anne had lived so
quietly in her home circle that few indeed in the
city knew anything of the treasure in their midst.

But the little family knew what they had lost,
for Anne's influence had been all-powerful with
those she loved. Mother, Mademoiselle, Jojo and
the two little ones, even the servants—she had
taken them all in her arms and carried them very
close to God. What she had done for their souls
was evident now that grief had come. Even the little ones were full of joy and surprisingly calm. They
said they felt that Nenette had not really gone but
come closer to them, even *inside*. There was no
fright of death.

One afternoon Jojo stayed beside the little white
form that had been his sister. He knelt there a long
time, leaning on the bed where she lay looking so
beautiful in the soft light of the candles. The little nine-year-old boy took no notice of anybody;
he seemed absorbed in a whispered conversation
with his sister. After a long time, Madame de
Guigné touched him on the shoulder and suggested
that he had been there long enough. "No,"
answered Jojo firmly, "I've lots more things to say
to Nenette," and he continued his conversation.

Sometime later an idea seemed to strike him. He
ran out of the room and went about the house col-
lecting everybody's prayerbooks and holy pictures
and brought them all down to Anne's room, where
he piled them in a heap beside the bed and then
proceeded to press each thing against her hand.

Madame de Guigné and Mademoiselle watched him in silent astonishment. They would hardly have dared to proclaim so boldly that their darling was a Saint, but the little boy looked round at them and said firmly: "Someday you will be very glad I have done this." And he went on making relics! They did not stop him; they watched through their tears, and the mother kept all these words in her heart.

Next came the children of the catechism class, those little girls who had all wanted to sit next to Anne "because she was the nicest." It is very remarkable what a lasting impression Anne had made on those children, for the memory of her example has not yet faded, after the lapse of several years. She had led them nearer to God, and she keeps them there.

"If I die, I will come and help you from Heaven," Anne had said to her own special friend, and she keeps her word. This child says that she can always count on Anne helping her to be good, and, "When I am in trouble I tell her about it first because I know she will comfort me and make me like her."

A few days later, Anne's body was taken home to Annecy-le-Vieux[2] and laid in the family vault.

She was not among strangers here, for the whole countryside knew the sweet little girl who had "prayed so well." That is how they described her, and they were not wrong. She had prayed well, and

---

2. The Chateau is near Annecy-le-Vieux (Old Annecy), some distance from the town of Annecy.

now in Heaven she was to pray still better, as her
own former neighbors were to be among the first
to find out.

*   *   *

Many striking cures have been attributed to
Anne's intercession during these few years that have
passed since her death. Some of these will be
described in due course, but first something must
be said about a few of the remarkable conversions
reported from all sides. Anne would wish it so, for
she loved her precious sinners so much on earth
that it was only to be expected she would help
them first when she came into her full power.

One of her first "big fishes" was an old grave-
digger of Annecy-le-Vieux, called Guste, a man
"of the earth, earthy"; one whose soul did not show
much sign of existence. He fell ill, however, with
no hope of recovery; and the Sisters who visited
him suggested that it was time to think of eternity. But Guste had no taste for such things. He
refused to see a priest or even to pray, so the nuns
thought it was a case for Anne. They remembered
how she had stormed Heaven for some of her "precious sinners" and would not be satisfied till the
soul was won, so now they put the case of this
sinner of her own parish before her and begged
her to see him safe into Heaven. Guste became
very bad not long after and both the parish priest
and his curate tried hard to win the old man to
make his peace with God, but in vain. Shortly
after, he lost consciousness. It seemed a hopeless

case, but both priests and sisters turned to little
Anne with renewed insistence. She must not let
one of her own old people die like a dog. "That
evening during Vespers," writes the nun who usually visited the family, "I felt a pressing inspiration to go back to the old man. To my amazement
I found him asking for the priest! In a short time
he was anointed and received holy Viaticum with
the fervor of an Angel."

At Vignère, a village near Annecy, there was an
old woman so deaf that she could not hear a word.
She fell ill, and when Father M. (curate of Annecy-
le-Vieux) came to administer the Last Sacraments,
he found her not only incapable of hearing, but
almost unconscious as well. What was to be done?
He pulled her bed nearer the window, hoping that
the light might rouse her; then he shook her gently. All to no purpose—the old woman remained
inert. "Then," says the priest, "it occurred to me
to invoke little Annette; so I prayed to her and
said a "Hail Mary." Immediately the sick woman
roused herself and answered all I asked her. I was
astonished, but since that day I know who to go
to in a difficulty."

One day in Annecy, Madame de Guigné was
called to assist a man who had been picked up terribly injured after an accident. He was quickly taken
to the hospital, but the doctors, though they
intended to operate immediately, said that there
was not the hundredth chance for him. Madame

de Guigné was much distressed, for she could not bear to think of a human soul being allowed to appear before God unprepared, and possibly in sin. The poor man was being prepared for the operation while she was imploring the nurses to let him see a priest first. But the case seemed hopeless, and the doctors were impatient. "Impossible, Madame. The man cannot speak, and he is never likely to speak. There is not a drop of blood left in his body."

"Oh yes, he will," answered Anne's mother, "but there is not a moment to lose." Where did she get such confidence? She had prayed to her little girl, and she felt sure Anne would do her utmost to prevent a soul going into eternity unprepared. She was right. Contrary to all expectation, the man soon recovered consciousness, made his Confession and followed the ceremonies of Extreme Unction attentively and with intelligence. Two hours later he died.

One of the most remarkable conversions that seem to be due to Anne's intercession was that of a young Bolshevist woman in 1925. The story is told by Rev. Fr. E. Lajeunie, O.P.[3]

"On March 25th, 1925, I went to hear the confessions of a community of nuns devoted to nursing. The Superioress asked me to come and see a young woman who was dying of rapid consumption. The patient was a communist who declared herself incapable of believing in God, though the nuns had done all they could to reach her soul and

---

3. The account has been condensed and shortened.

she had studied religion carefully. It did not sound hopeful. Was I likely to succeed where so many others had failed? I was tired too and felt no confidence, for the Bolshevist had made up her mind not to be persuaded. The prospect was not cheerful, but suddenly I thought of Anne and earnestly begged her to convert this soul for me.

"The invalid was no ordinary woman, I could see that at a glance. Energy, pride and an unusual frankness were written in every line of the fine head and face; loyalty and keen intelligence in the clear eyes. She told me her story in calm, simple and very decided words. There was no sorrow for her past, she was proud of it. 'I have no faith,' she said. 'I would like to believe, but I cannot. I have studied religion deeply but it does not touch me. I cannot believe in the Divinity of Christ.'

"It seems that she had made her First Communion as a child, but had seized the truths of faith only with her mind and not with her heart. Then she went to school, a godless school; then to the University and finally to England for further studies, against her parents' wishes. In order to make her return, they stopped her allowance; but being very tenacious in her purposes, she started to give classes to support herself. Communism interested her greatly and she finally became an avowed follower of the doctrines of Lenin. This interest led her, as might be expected, into Bolshevist circles, and before long she married a Russian, out of the Church of course. He was a notorious revolutionary who had been condemned to death several times, and now she also took part in many Bolshevist activities, carrying out more than one perilous mission with remarkable audacity and intelligence.

"But now all that was over. She was near death, laid low by a relentless illness, but with a mind as firmly set in her own convictions as ever it had been. To convert her needed a miracle of grace, for all the powers of her clear intelligence were deliberately concentrated on a chosen ideal. She would perhaps *add* the Gospel to the doctrines of Lenin, but she had no idea of denying Bolshevism to adore Christ. It seemed a hopeless case, for sins of the intelligence are the most subtle, the most grave and the most invincible. Interiorly, I called more and more earnestly to Anne, for I felt God might grant this grace through her intercession. Nor was I wrong. I said only a few words, reminding the poor woman that she had received the Faith in Baptism and that if she now asked pardon God would give her faith and pardon. She was silent a moment, looking troubled and distressed. Then to my amazement she suddenly said: 'Yes, I will confess my sins,' and began to accuse herself. It was indeed a miracle, for her heart was completely changed in those few moments. She received Holy Communion the next day and every day after that with the greatest fervor. But she still clung to life until Good Friday came, then she rose to the full height of what God asked of her and offered Him the sacrifice of her life. From that day she only wished to suffer or to die in expiation of her sins, and to obtain the conversion of her family.

"She soon learned to love little Anne, and also
St. Thérèse of Lisieux, whose death she was about
to share, for all the terrible sufferings which frequently accompany the illness now fell on the
young convert, and she bore them like a saint. On
July 4, she received the Last Sacraments with great
joy. During that night she seemed to be going
through a tragic struggle with the powers of dark-
ness, but after some time she fixed her eyes on the
statue of St. Thérèse with a look of joy and then
apparently followed something round the room,
murmuring: 'Thérèse.' But it was only a momen-
tary ray of light, for the combat recommenced.
Then again her face lightened and she looked this
time at the statue of Our Lady, saying: 'Oh, isn't
she beautiful?' The Queen of Heaven had brought
relief to her soul, if not to her body. Peace reigned
in her heart now until the end, though the agony
was to continue for some hours yet. As the morning came she cried out: 'Jesus, come and fetch me.
Oh, come and fetch me!' Then: 'Father, Mother,
come . . .' and she held out her arms. Then: 'Jesus!'
and she was gone. Such was Anne's convert."

On January 18, 1925, the following letter arrived:
". . . Being somewhat skeptical after reading the
life of little Anne, which I thought rather forced,
I asked her to give me confidence in her sanctity
by a miracle. It was a bit of audacity on my part,
but evidently she was not offended, since she has
answered me almost immediately. A few days later
I paid a visit to my own people and happened to

go and see a young man who had been suffering
for six years with tuberculosis, enduring much but
without faith. I felt very anxious about him, but it
was impossible to speak about religion because he
was so opposed to the subject. The thought of Anne
came into my mind, and so I prayed to her for this
conversion. The next day I left the town but continued to beg her to save this soul. Well, yesterday what was my surprise to find a letter from my
mother telling me: 'Poor L. . . wants you to know
that on Thursday evening he asked for a priest of
his own accord, went to Confession and received
Holy Communion on Friday morning! He told his
mother that his conscience is now at rest and he
is glad to die like a Christian so that God will
receive him into Heaven.' Could I ask more? Why
had the poor boy wanted me specially to know that
he was converted? Why should he ask them to tell
me, if it was not that Anne wanted me to have
the sign I had asked for?"

Another time it was an old Freemason, who had
been received into a home kept by nuns but
remained utterly unconverted; in fact, he would not
stop swearing and blaspheming whenever he saw a
priest enter the room. But the nuns gave the old
sinner a picture of Anne, and at the very sight of
it he was suddenly touched by grace and soon after
went to Confession.

But it is not only big sinners that Anne loves.
In Heaven as on earth, she is still the "Apostle of

the Nursery." While she was alive there were not many whom she could lead to God—just her own brother and sisters and a few playmates. Now, however, her circle of friends is very much larger. Anne has become the "children's Apostle," and she is casting her nets far into the deep.

Here is one story among many. A young girl who had come to love Nenette after reading her life was very anxious about a little girl whose parents were careless Catholics. The poor child went to a non-Catholic school and knew next to nothing about religion. However, it was arranged that she should be prepared for her First Communion, and her young friend managed to get her into a convent school for a time. She then started praying to Anne for the little one, begging her to win this soul for God. At first she thought Anne was rather deaf to her prayers for the child seemed so indifferent about religion; nothing could touch her heart, apparently. She did not at all like going to church, and though she made some sort of effort to prepare for the great act, she did not seem to care much and her friend became rather anxious for fear the child might not make a good First Communion. "I simply begged dear little Anne to change her heart," the girl wrote, "and I asked God to give me a sign so that I might know she had made a good Communion. It was June 1, 1926. The child certainly looked like an angel that morning, and in the evening she came up to me and pointed to her heart, saying: "Jesus is there and I will not let Him go." She repeated this three times. Wasn't it the sign I had asked for? I thought it was enough certainly, but Anne did more than that, for the very next day the child's mother and father went to Confession, which they had not done for twelve years, as they had completely given up all practice of their religion." It may be as well to add that the little girl has kept to the grace of her First Communion and is now a good child.

Another who was described as "a terrible child" happened to read Anne's life and was transformed by it. "She lost her mother some time ago," a friend wrote, "and did not seem to care much about it. She was a terrible child whose only ambition was to be either an actress or a witch! . . . Now, since reading that life she is completely changed. She asked someone if she could become like Anne if she prayed to her. Then she made a novena, and we have seen the result."

Anne also continues her work of drawing souls to the special service of God. She wants many others besides that one little friend whom she knew on earth to "take her place in a convent."

Here is a striking story. A young girl who longed to be a nun was prevented from following her vocation by the opposition of her mother, who absolutely refused her consent. "I prayed continually to little Anne," the girl writes, "and she has at last helped me. This morning Mother was quite changed. We had a terrible scene last night, for Mother tried to make me promise to stay with her.

Of course I could not promise and I went upstairs broken-hearted. Almost in despair, I begged Anne to 'arrange things' as she used to do on earth, and now Mother is quite resigned about my leaving her and is so calm. I am so happy, I feel inclined to sing the Magnificat."

Another of Anne's disciples was a young man who loved to "see life," as the saying is. But he had not long to enjoy himself. At eighteen he fell ill without hope of recovery. Fortunately, he had a mother who confided the care of his soul as well as his body to Nenette, whose relic he wore.

It was a work worthy of Anne, and she did what we might have expected of her. She transformed his heart completely, and he accepted the sentence of death with real joy. Earthly pleasures were no longer an attraction. His one desire now, if God should give him life, was to spend it in His service as a priest. But this was not to be. Anne came to fetch him.

There are plenty of other stories of the same kind, but an account must now be given of a few of the cures that appear to be miraculous.

Perhaps one of the most remarkable is the case of a young girl suffering from purulent pleurisy, who was suddenly cured after praying to Anne. Her illness was palpably evident to those who nursed her, and the cure is certified by radiography and the testimony of three doctors and several witnesses.

The Superioress General of a congregation of Dominican nuns writes: "One of our nuns, the Prioress of the convent at B. . . had an accident which seriously injured her eye. She could not see and suffered atrociously. I had sent her one of the little relics of Anne, which she laid upon her eye and was then able to sleep. On waking she found to her astonishment that all pain was gone. She could open the wounded eye and see with it as well as the other. The oculist considers that this sudden change is truly extraordinary."

A mother writes: "My son had a terrible fall from a horse. He was picked up unconscious and was in danger for several days. His sight was gone on account of hemorrhage in the retina and other complications. The doctor declared that he would never be able to see again. His career seemed to be ruined, but on October 18 (three weeks after the accident), while we were making novena after novena to little Anne, he wrote to me, saying: 'I cannot think how it happened, but the day before yesterday I found I could recognize people at a distance of more than four yards, though before that I could not even distinguish the shape of anyone a yard off.' The little Saint has continued her prayers, for his eyes are getting steadily better. . . ."

Another letter: "My sister, a medical student, had read the life of Anne de Guigné and we discussed it at some length, for she could not believe so young a child could be a Saint. Now the day after this discussion my sister was taken suddenly very ill with diphtheria. . . It was impossible for me to get a doctor then, for it was during the early hours of the morning. I did not know what to do, so I prayed to little Anne and begged my sister to do the same. At once the swelling ceased and there was no immediate danger. As soon as it was possible, of course, we got the doctor, who did everything he could for her, but I firmly believe that it was the prayers of that blessed child which saved her."

This belief seems justified to those who know how swiftly diphtheria can be fatal when no medical aid is to be had.

A missionary student writes: "One of my nephews, aged three months, became suddenly very ill. The doctor found two large abscesses which he opened—after considerable hesitation—because he was afraid the little boy was too weak to stand the operation; but it was obviously necessary, for the child's blood was being poisoned by the abscess. In a few hours it would have been too late.

"The night of August 23 passed uneventfully; but the next day about twelve o'clock, Regis refused all food, his temperature was 106° and his breathing became irregular. At 5 p.m. when I came in from a visit to the church, I found everyone in despair. 'There is no hope for him now,' I was told. The poor child was lying with half-shut eyes, looking quite lifeless, his face waxen as a corpse. About 9 p.m. the rattle commenced. We were all kneeling around the bed, expecting the end, when I

thought of invoking Anne de Guigné. I begged her
to use all her power with God to save my little
nephew, and I put a picture of her on his chest.
Then I went to bed feeling hopeful. The next morning I found the little boy had returned to life. They
told me a sudden change had occurred. Since then
he has gotten quite well and is so at present."

In January 1925, Marinette, Anne's little sister,
became seriously ill with influenza. Her temperature rose to 103° and remained there, while the
state of her pulse caused anxiety. One evening she
appeared to be much worse, and the feverish rest-
lessness increased. Madame de Guigné then put a
little piece of Nenette's linen under the little one's
pillow and prayed to her eldest child. Immediately,
under her eyes, Marinette became calm, the rapid
breathing more natural and the little girl fell asleep.
The next day her temperature had fallen to 99.5°,
and convalescence followed.

That same January, a great friend of her mother's,
whom Anne used to call "Aunt Paula," was also
down with a "flu." For three days she was very bad
and finally phoned Madame de Guigné in a most
depressed frame of mind. "I am so bad," she said,
"my temperature goes on rising and I can't do anything. It really frightens me to be ill like this. Physically and morally I feel at the end of things."
Madame de Guigné was much distressed and turned
as usual to her little girl. Might not a mother command her child even in Heaven? "Nenette," she

said, "you really *must* make poor Aunt Paula better, at once!" About 4 p.m. the phone rang again. It was Aunt Paula, speaking in her normal voice. "I am extraordinarily better," she said. "I don't know what has happened, but I feel a different person altogether." Madame de Guigné smiled. "When did you feel better?" "About a quarter of an hour after I spoke to you. I believe our Nenette has done it."

Like Our Lady of Lourdes, Anne does not always cure her protegés, but answers their prayers by teaching them the value of suffering cheerfully borne for God's sake. To cure the soul is a greater thing than to cure the body. This was the lesson she taught to the mother of two Carmelite nuns, who had made novena after novena to be cured, but became very much worse. There was a change in her soul, however, for she realized that Christ had called her to share His Cross, and with the realization came the grace to accept His Will in the spirit of St. Thérèse.

Anne came herself to fetch one whom God did not wish her to cure. The young woman was seriously ill with bronchial pneumonia, but not at all in a hopeless condition. When the critical stage was reached, her relatives put a picture of Anne on her pillow and began to pray earnestly, the patient joining in with touching fervor. The next day she seemed to be much better in every way. She was very bright and they thought Anne had answered their prayers. She had indeed, but in

God's way. That afternoon, when the nun who had told them about Anne came to see the invalid, this latter related what had really happened.

She said she had seen an Angel under the form of a wonderfully beautiful little girl who smiled at her. For a moment she thought it must be her own child who had died a few years before; but after a moment's thought she felt certain that it was Anne de Guigné. While the little girl stood smiling at her, there came a sound of music too sweet for this world and she knew that Anne had come to fetch her. From this moment the invalid prepared for death, much to the astonishment of her family, who thought her better. She insisted on seeing her confessor and begged him to give her the Last Sacraments, but he hesitated because the doctor did not think there was any great danger and the patient seemed likely to recover. That evening her parents came to say goodnight. "Oh, don't leave me," she said. "But why not?" asked her mother, "you are not so bad now, dear, and the nurse is here." "Oh, very well," sighed the invalid, "you won't see me again though, or rather, you *will* see me, but I shall be dead." She was right, for a few minutes later she died. Anne knew better than the doctors.

There are other favors of all sorts to record, for Anne is quite as kind-hearted in Heaven as she was on earth and she gives her clients what they ask if it will "make them good"! Now, as always, she thinks first of those things that will add to "the glory of God," so her own dear old parish priest of

Annecy-le-Vieux knew very well he could count
upon her help in restoring the parish church. He
started without any money, trusting Anne to
"arrange things" for him; nor was he disappointed.
In a very short time 29,000 francs found their way
into his purse, one way or another, though the little parish is quite poor. He often says: "I know my
little Anne is a Saint, because she gives me everything I ask for!"

The Franciscan Missionaries of Mary were very
devoted to Anne, whose great-grandmother and
great-aunts were among their foundresses. Two of
these sisters who were trying to sell the work done
by their orphan girls put their business under
Anne's protection, begging her to see that all their
wares would bring a good price. Though at first
they had not much luck, they boldly asked their
little patroness to let them get 1500 francs at a
certain ladies' boarding house where they seldom
got more than about 400 francs. Their confidence
was not deceived, for this time the ladies bought
goods to the value of 1600 francs! Encouraged by
this success, the Sisters went on praying and got
5000 francs in three days, which was far more than
usual. Finally, everything they had with them was
sold except a very beautiful (and very expensive!)
baptismal robe. But the Sisters trusted Anne,
though they felt a little disappointed because she
had not helped them to dispose of their most valu-
able piece of work, and they told her so, perhaps
a bit impatiently. There is no time in Heaven, how-

ever, and the Saints do not mind making us wait
a little. In this case, Anne only tested their faith
for a very short time. They had scarcely gotten back
that evening when a lady rang them up and said
she would like to buy the baptismal robe!

Here is another story of Anne's kindness. "For
years, owing to money losses, I have been obliged
to work continually to support my mother and
invalid sisters. After eighteen years of this in addi-
tion to housework, my health gave way and the
doctor insisted on two or three months of absolute
rest. What was to be done? I put the whole matter into Anne's hands. 'You see, dear little Anne,'
I said to her, 'I have done all I can, now won't you
see to things?' After that I felt at peace and did
not worry any more.

"The next day an old friend of my family called
and gave me a large sum of money, quite enough
to live on for three months! He said he had been
so strongly impelled to come and give it to me that
he felt sure it was an inspiration from Heaven. 'I
felt an interior force,' he said, 'which made me take
the first train to come and help you.' Surely this
irresistible force was my dear little Anne, for I had
put the matter in her hands and no one else knew
of my trouble, not even my mother."

Another time she found a good job for the father
of a poor family, and then she settled a painful law-
suit for someone else.

"I left my purse on a shop counter," writes another lady, "and went back hours later, not hoping to find it, for the shop had been full of people that day. But I prayed to Anne and there it was, just where I had left it beside the door, with crowds of people passing every moment."

And so it goes on; from all sides a chorus of grateful voices rise up calling the little one "blessed." May the day soon come when the Church will repeat in the name of God what those who knew Anne said as she passed from this world: "She is a Saint!"

AFTERWORD
Added by the Publisher in 1997*

In 1932 the Bishop of Annecy, Msgr. du Bois' de la Villerabel, opened the canonical investigation into Anne's life and virtues; he designated October 30, 1933 for the exhumation of her remains. On that day the canonical examination of the remains took place in the presence of the Bishop, two priests of the cathedral, two nuns, doctors, Anne's mother, other relatives and the appointed workmen. The examination took place according to a formal protocol. Before the casket was removed from the vault, all present had to take a solemn oath on the Gospels not to declare anything except the exact truth about what was to take place.

The casket was removed from the family vault and brought in procession, with prayers, into the Guigné home. The Bishop threatened with excommunication anyone who would take even the smallest piece from the casket or its contents or add

---

*Most of this Afterword originally came from a German book by Fr. Dr. Albert Wihler entitled *"Nichts ist schwer, wenn man GOTT lieb hat"*—*Anna de Guigné (1911-1922)*, copyright © 1981 (7th edition) by the publisher: Freundeskreis Maria Goretti e.V., Planegger Strasse 22b, D-81241 München.

anything to it. He then ordered the casket to be opened.

When the casket was opened, the body was found to be preserved intact. Those present who had known Anne found her features exactly as before. All were filled with a respectful amazement.

Then the Bishop gave the order for the doctors to conduct their examination. The doctors determined that the body was not decayed. They lifted it out of the casket by the neck and feet, temporarily placing it on a cloth-covered table. The two nuns present decorated a new casket with white satin cloth, then the doctors placed the body therein, and the Bishop placed in the casket a document signed by several witnesses. Madame de Guigné asked the Bishop's permission to touch the Rosary beads in the hands of the little angel, and the Bishop granted her request.

Meanwhile about 300 people had been waiting outside in the cold rain and icy wind for over an hour. They were now allowed to come in and file past the body in silence. Two priests stood by to touch the casket with any article the people handed them as a memento. Then the casket was sealed with six seals to signify that this body now belonged to Holy Church. The casket was placed inside another casket which was locked and sealed by the city council, then brought back in procession and locked in the vault. The people, deeply moved, silently took their leave, and the Bishop bid the family good-bye with the words: "We'll meet again at the beatification!"

The story of Anne de Guigné has spread far and wide. By 1956 there had been close to 50 books written about her in over 20 languages, including Chinese, Japanese and Arabic.

In 1955 a Postulator was appointed in Rome to begin the beatification process. But like many other causes of children and youths, the process became stalled until 1983, when new procedures for beatification were introduced.

The cause of Anne de Guigné took a big step forward when Pope John Paul II approved a decree on March 3, 1990 recognizing her Heroic Virtue. Before this decree was possible there had been a long discussion on the question whether children from age 7-14 were capable of practicing the virtues in an extraordinary, heroic way. This question was finally decided in the affirmative, and the decree was approved. In the decree the Holy Father stated:

"We ascertain that the Servant of God, Anne de Guigné, has really practiced in a heroic manner the Theological Virtues of Faith, Hope and Charity—the last-named being practiced toward God and neighbor—and the Cardinal Virtues of Prudence, Justice, Temperance and Fortitude, as well as the other virtues connected with these."

As the next step toward beatification, a miracle is required—a miracle worked by God through Anne's intercession, officially witnessed, and then approved by the Church.

Information regarding special favors obtained through Anne's intercession may be sent to the

Postulator of her cause:

> Fr. Nicolas Hedreul-Tanoarn, O.P.
> 94 via Germanico,
> I-00192 ROMA
> Italia

Anne's sister Marinette is a Dominican sister. One may write to her for picture cards of Anne:

> Soeur Anne de Saint-Jacques, O.P.
> Soeurs Dominicaines,
> Villa Saint Benoit
> 16, Avenue Isola Bella
> F-06400 CANNES
> France

There is also a French association called "Friends of Anne de Guigné":

> Association des Amis Anne de Guigné
> 11 rue Weber
> F-75116 PARIS
> France

PRAYER
To Obtain the Glorification of
Ven. Anne de Guigné

O JESUS, full of grace and charity, and so merciful to all who call upon Thee, I humbly beseech Thee to glorify in Heaven and on earth the Servant of God, Venerable Anne de Guigné, who loved Thee so much and who was always ready to offer prayers and sacrifices for the glory of God and the good of souls.

With confidence I beseech Thee to grant me, through her intercession, the grace of (*state your petition*), which I ardently desire.

Glory be to the Father . . . (*three times*).

Imprimatur:

✠ Most Rev. Thomas G. Doran, D.D., J.C.D.
Bishop of Rockford
August 18, 1997

If you have enjoyed this book, consider making your next selection from among the following . . .

Prices subject to change.

Stories of Padre Pio. *Tangari* 8.00
Miraculous Images of Our Lady. *Joan Carroll Cruz* 20.00
Miraculous Images of Our Lord. *Cruz* 13.50
Brief Catechism for Adults. *Fr. Cogan* 9.00
Raised from the Dead. *Fr. Hebert* 16.50
Autobiography of St. Margaret Mary 6.00
Thoughts and Sayings of St. Margaret Mary 5.00
The Voice of the Saints. *Comp. by Francis Johnston* 7.00
The 12 Steps to Holiness and Salvation. *St. Alphonsus* 7.50
The Rosary and the Crisis of Faith. *Cirrincione/Nelson* 2.00
Sin and Its Consequences. *Cardinal Manning* 7.00
St. Francis of Paola. *Simi & Segreti* 8.00
Dialogue of St. Catherine of Siena. *Transl. Thorold* 10.00
Catholic Answer to Jehovah's Witnesses. *D'Angelo* 12.00
Twelve Promises of the Sacred Heart. (100 cards) 5.00
Life of St. Aloysius Gonzaga. *Fr. Meschler* 12.00
The Love of Mary. *D. Roberto* 8.00
Begone Satan. *Fr. Vogl* 3.00
The Prophets and Our Times. *Fr. R. G. Culleton* 13.50
St. Therese, The Little Flower. *John Beevers* 6.00
Mary, The Second Eve. *Cardinal Newman* 3.00
Devotion to Infant Jesus of Prague. *Booklet* 75
The Wonder of Guadalupe. *Francis Johnston* 7.50
Apologetics. *Msgr. Paul Glenn* 10.00
Baltimore Catechism No. 1 . . . . 3.50
Baltimore Catechism No. 2 . . . . 4.50
Baltimore Catechism No. 3 . . . . 8.00
An Explanation of the Baltimore Catechism. *Kinkead*. 16.50
Bible History. *Schuster* 13.50
Blessed Eucharist. *Fr. Mueller* 9.00
Catholic Catechism. *Fr. Faerber* 7.00
The Devil. *Fr. Delaporte* 6.00
Dogmatic Theology for the Laity. *Fr. Premm* 20.00
Evidence of Satan in the Modern World. *Cristiani* 10.00
Fifteen Promises of Mary. (100 cards) 5.00
Life of Anne Catherine Emmerich. 2 vols. *Schmoeger* 37.50
Life of the Blessed Virgin Mary. *Emmerich* 16.50
Prayer to St. Michael. (100 leaflets). 5.00
Prayerbook of Favorite Litanies. *Fr. Hebert* 10.00
Preparation for Death. (Abridged). *St. Alphonsus* 8.00
Purgatory Explained. *Schouppe* 13.50
Purgatory Explained. (pocket, unabr.). *Schouppe* 9.00
Spiritual Conferences. *Tauler* 13.00
Trustful Surrender to Divine Providence. *Bl. Claude*. 5.00

Prices subject to change.

Forty Dreams of St. John Bosco. *Bosco* 12.50
Blessed Miguel Pro. *Ball* 6.00
Soul Sanctified. *Anonymous* 9.00
Wife, Mother and Mystic. *Bessieres* 8.00
The Agony of Jesus. *Padre Pio* 2.00
Catholic Home Schooling. *Mary Kay Clark* 18.00
The Cath. Religion—Illus. & Expl. *Msgr. Burbach* 9.00
Wonders of the Holy Name. *Fr. O'Sullivan* 1.50
How Christ Said the First Mass. *Fr. Meagher* 18.50
Too Busy for God? Think Again! *D'Angelo* 5.00
St. Bernadette Soubirous. *Trochu* 18.50
Passion and Death of Jesus Christ. *Liguori* 10.00
Life Everlasting. *Garrigou-Lagrange* 13.50
Confession Quizzes. *Radio Replies Press* 1.50
St. Philip Neri. *Fr. V. J. Matthews* 5.50
St. Louise de Marillac. *Sr. Vincent Regnault* 6.00
The Old World and America. *Rev. Philip Furlong* 18.00
Prophecy for Today. *Edward Connor* 5.50
Bethlehem. *Fr. Faber* 18.00
The Book of Infinite Love. *Mother de la Touche* 5.00
The Church Teaches. *Church Documents* 16.50
Conversation with Christ. *Peter T. Rohrbach* 10.00
Purgatory and Heaven. *J. P. Arendzen* 5.00
Liberalism Is a Sin. *Sarda y Salvany* 7.50
Spiritual Legacy/Sr. Mary of Trinity. *van den Broek* 10.00
The Creator and the Creature. *Fr. Frederick Faber* 16.50
Radio Replies. 3 Vols. *Frs. Rumble and Carty* 42.00
Convert's Catechism of Catholic Doctrine. *Geiermann* 3.00
Incarnation, Birth, Infancy of Jesus Christ. *Liguori* 10.00
Light and Peace. *Fr. R. P. Quadrupani* 7.00
Dogmatic Canons & Decrees of Trent, Vat. I 9.50
The Evolution Hoax Exposed. *A. N. Field* 7.50
The Priest, the Man of God. *St. Joseph Cafasso* 13.50
Christ Denied. *Fr. Paul Wickens* 2.50
New Regulations on Indulgences. *Fr. Winfrid Herbst* 2.50
A Tour of the Summa. *Msgr. Paul Glenn* 18.00
Spiritual Conferences. *Fr. Frederick Faber* 15.00
Bible Quizzes. *Radio Replies Press* 1.50
Marriage Quizzes. *Radio Replies Press* 1.50
True Church Quizzes. *Radio Replies Press* 1.50
Mary, Mother of the Church. *Church Documents* 4.00
The Sacred Heart and the Priesthood. *de la Touche* 9.00
Blessed Sacrament. *Fr. Faber* 18.50
Revelations of St. Bridget. *St. Bridget of Sweden* 3.00

Prices subject to change.

Story of a Soul. *St. Therese of Lisieux*................. 8.00
Catholic Children's Treasure Box Books 1-10............ 35.00
Prayers and Heavenly Promises. *Cruz*................. 5.00
Magnificent Prayers. *St. Bridget of Sweden*........... 2.00
The Happiness of Heaven. *Fr. J. Boudreau*............ 8.00
The Holy Eucharist—Our All. *Fr. Lucas Etlin*......... 2.00
The Glories of Mary. *St. Alphonsus Liguori*........... 16.50
The Curé D'Ars. *Abbé Francis Trochu*................ 21.50
Humility of Heart. *Fr. Cajetan da Bergamo*........... 8.50
Love, Peace and Joy. (St. Gertrude). *Prévot*.......... 7.00
Père Lamy. *Biver*................................. 12.00
Passion of Jesus & Its Hidden Meaning. *Groenings*...... 15.00
Mother of God & Her Glorious Feasts. *Fr. O'Laverty*... 10.00
Song of Songs—A Mystical Exposition. *Fr. Arintero*... 20.00
Love and Service of God, Infinite Love. *de la Touche*... 12.50
Life & Work of Mother Louise Marg. *Fr. O'Connell*.... 12.50
Martyrs of the Coliseum. *O'Reilly*.................. 18.50
Rhine Flows into the Tiber. *Fr. Wiltgen*.............. 15.00
What Catholics Believe. *Fr. Lawrence Lovasik*......... 5.00
Who Is Therese Neumann? *Fr. Charles Carty*.......... 2.00
Summa of the Christian Life. 3 Vols. *Granada*......... 36.00
St. Francis of Paola. *Simi and Segreti*............... 8.00
The Rosary in Action. *John Johnson*................. 9.00
St. Dominic. *Sr. Mary Jean Dorcy*.................. 10.00
Is It a Saint's Name? *Fr. William Dunne*............. 2.50
St. Martin de Porres. *Giuliana Cavallini*............. 12.50
Douay-Rheims New Testament. *Paperbound*........... 15.00
St. Catherine of Siena. *Alice Curtayne*.............. 13.50
Blessed Virgin Mary. *Liguori*...................... 6.00
Chats With Converts. *Fr. M. D. Forrest*.............. 10.00
The Stigmata and Modern Science. *Fr. Charles Carty*.... 1.50
St. Gertrude the Great............................. 1.50
Thirty Favorite Novenas........................... .75
Brief Life of Christ. *Fr. Rumble*................... 2.00
Catechism of Mental Prayer. *Msgr. Simler*............ 2.00
On Freemasonry. *Pope Leo XIII*.................... 1.50
Thoughts of the Curé D'Ars. *St. John Vianney*........ 2.00
Incredible Creed of Jehovah Witnesses. *Fr. Rumble*..... 1.50
St. Pius V—His Life, Times, Miracles. *Anderson*....... 5.00
St. Dominic's Family. *Sr. Mary Jean Dorcy*........... 24.00
St. Rose of Lima. *Sr. Alphonsus*................... 15.00
Latin Grammar. *Scanlon & Scanlon*................. 16.50
Second Latin. *Scanlon & Scanlon*.................. 12.00
St. Joseph of Copertino. *Pastrovicchi*............... 6.00

Prices subject to change.

Saint Michael and the Angels. *Approved Sources* 7.00
Dolorous Passion of Our Lord. *Anne C. Emmerich* 16.50
Our Lady of Fatima's Peace Plan from Heaven. *Booklet* 75
Three Ways of the Spiritual Life. *Garrigou-Lagrange.* 6.00
Mystical Evolution. 2 Vols. *Fr. Arintero, O.P.* 36.00
St. Catherine Labouré of the Mirac. Medal. *Fr. Dirvin* 13.50
Manual of Practical Devotion to St. Joseph. *Patrignani.* 15.00
The Active Catholic. *Fr. Palau* 7.00
Ven. Jacinta Marto of Fatima. *Cirrincione* 2.00
Reign of Christ the King. *Davies* 1.25
St. Teresa of Avila. *William Thomas Walsh* 21.50
Isabella of Spain—The Last Crusader. *Wm. T. Walsh* 20.00
Characters of the Inquisition. *Wm. T. Walsh* 15.00
Philip II. *William Thomas Walsh.* HB. 37.50
Blood-Drenched Altars—Cath. Comment. Hist. Mexico 20.00
Self-Abandonment to Divine Providence. *de Caussade.* 18.00
Way of the Cross. *Liguorian.* 1.00
Way of the Cross. *Franciscan.* 1.00
Modern Saints—Their Lives & Faces, Bk. 1. *Ann Ball* 18.00
Modern Saints—Their Lives & Faces, Bk. 2. *Ann Ball* 20.00
Divine Favors Granted to St. Joseph. *Pere Binet* 5.00
St. Joseph Cafasso—Priest of the Gallows. *St. J. Bosco* 5.00
Catechism of the Council of Trent. *McHugh/Callan* 24.00
Why Squander Illness? *Frs. Rumble & Carty* 2.50
Fatima—The Great Sign. *Francis Johnston.* 8.00
Heliotropium—Conformity of Human Will to Divine 13.00
Charity for the Suffering Souls. *Fr. John Nageleisen.* 16.50
Devotion to the Sacred Heart of Jesus. *Verheylezoon* 15.00
Sermons on Prayer. *St. Francis de Sales* 4.00
Sermons on Our Lady. *St. Francis de Sales.* 10.00
Sermons for Lent. *St. Francis de Sales* 12.00
Fundamentals of Catholic Dogma. *Ott* 21.00
Litany of the Blessed Virgin Mary. (100 cards) 5.00
Who Is Padre Pio? *Radio Replies Press* 2.00
Child's Bible History. *Knecht* 5.00
The Life of Christ. 4 Vols. H.B. *Anne C. Emmerich* 60.00
St. Anthony—The Wonder Worker of Padua. *Stoddard* 5.00
The Precious Blood. *Fr. Faber* 13.50
The Holy Shroud & Four Visions. *Fr. O'Connell* 2.00
Clean Love in Courtship. *Fr. Lawrence Lovasik* 2.50
The Secret of the Rosary. *St. Louis De Montfort* 5.00

At your Bookdealer or direct from the Publisher.
Call Toll Free 1-800-437-5876

Prices subject to change.